FabJob Guide to
Become a Party Planner

JACKIE LARSON, CRAIG COOLAHAN
AND JENNIFER JAMES

FABJOB® GUIDE TO BECOME A PARTY PLANNER
by Jackie Larson, Craig Coolahan and Jennifer James

ISBN: 978-1-894638-92-0

Library and Archives Canada Cataloguing in Publication

Larson, Jackie
FabJob guide to become a party planner / by Jackie Larson,
Craig Coolahan and Jennifer James.

Includes bibliographical references.
ISBN: 978-1-894638-92-0

1. Parties—Planning. 2. Vocational guidance. I. James, Jennifer
II. Coolahan, Craig III. Title. IV. Title: Become a party planner.

GV1471.L37 2006   793.2'023   C2006-900090-5

Important Disclaimer: Although every effort has been made to ensure this guide is free from errors, this publication is sold with the understanding that the authors, editors, and publisher are not responsible for the results of any action taken on the basis of information in this work, nor for any errors or omissions. The publishers, and the authors and editors, expressly disclaim all and any liability to any person, whether a purchaser of this publication or not, in respect of anything and of the consequences of anything done or omitted to be done by any such person in reliance, whether whole or partial, upon the whole or any part of the contents of this publication. If expert advice is required, services of a competent professional person should be sought.

About the Websites Mentioned in this Guide: Although we aim to provide the information you need within the guide, we have also included a number of websites because readers have told us they appreciate knowing about sources of additional information. (**TIP:** Don't include a period at the end of a web address when you type it into your browser.) Due to the constant development of the Internet, websites can change. Any websites mentioned in this guide are included for the convenience of readers only. We are not responsible for the content of any sites except FabJob.com.

FabJob Inc.
19 Horizon View Court
Calgary, Alberta, Canada T3Z 3M5

FabJob Inc.
4616 25th Avenue NE, #224
Seattle, Washington, USA 98105

To order books in bulk, phone 403-949-2039
To arrange a media interview, phone 403-949-4980

www.FabJob.com
THE DREAM CAREER EXPERTS

Contents

About the Authors

Jackie Larson is a nationally published author whose business-related articles have appeared at MSNBC.com, AOL Small Business, Entrepreneur.com, and in the *Dallas Morning News*. She is a former Director of Public Relations who contributed to statewide marketing campaigns, and was also Editor-in-Chief of a group of regional magazines. She currently offers writing, copywriting and marketing services, and is based in Ennis, Texas. She can be reached at **jk_larson@hotmail.com**.

Craig Coolahan is a freelance writer and editor with degrees in English literature and journalism. Following stints as a reporter and as a communications coordinator, he set out to make a living freelancing, and has never looked back. The author of the *FabJob Guide to Become a Business Consultant*, Craig has contributed to several FabJob titles, and particularly enjoyed interviewing the "party animals" for this book. He lives and works in Calgary, Alberta, Canada, with his partner, Jackie, and children, Danielle and Jared.

About the Editor

Jennifer James leads the editorial department at FabJob Inc., the world's leading publisher of information about dream careers. She has edited, researched for, and contributed to more than 50 FabJob career guides, including the *FabJob Guide to Become a Makeup Artist*, the *FabJob Guide to Become a Professional Organizer*, and the *FabJob Guide to Become a Fashion Designer*, as well as the Amazon.com bestseller *Dream Careers* by Tag and Catherine Goulet.

Contributing Authors

Caryne Brown is an editorial consultant and business planner based in Los Angeles. As Senior Editor of *Entrepreneur* magazine, she wrote or supervised editing of more than 60 how-to books, and developed distance-learning courses in business planning and entrepreneurial management. Topics of business manuals she has written include start-up basics and increasing sales. As the "Ask the Experts" columnist for *Income Opportunities Magazine*, she answered reader inquiries on small business management. She was a founding editor of *Woman's Enterprise*, and her numerous other writing credits include *American History*, *Architectural Digest*, *Bon Appétit*, *Ironman*, and *Shape*.

Susan Wessling is an award-winning writer and editor whose work has been recognized by the National Newspaper Association (U.S.) and The New England Press Association. Her articles have appeared in a number of New England newspapers, U.S. and international magazines, and numerous education, health, and sports websites, including *Encyclopaedia Britannica's* online encyclopedia. Wessling lives in central Massachusetts with her partner Pat, their son Stephen, and Irish setter Clancy.

Acknowledgments

The FabJob editorial department and the authors of this book greatly appreciate the contributions of the following professional party planners and party industry experts, without whom this book would not have been possible.

An extra-special thanks goes to **Kathleen Kellner** of Eventful Productions in Calgary, Alberta, who took time out of her busy schedule to share insights with several FabJob authors for this guide.

Cheers!

- *Teresa Choate*
  At Its Best Events
  Waxahachie, TX

- *Sandra Dingler*
  Party Service Dallas
  Dallas, TX
  www.partyservicedallas.com

- *Debbie Donley*
  The Little Guest
  Solvang, CA
  www.syv.com/thelittleguest

- *Howard Feiertag*
  Department of Hospitality and Tourism Management,
  Virginia Polytechnic Institute and State University
  Blacksburg, VA

- *Jill Hawkins*
  Miller-Hawkins Productions
  Los Angeles, CA
  www.amillerhawkinsproduction.com

- *Heidi Hiller*
  Zozzie and Heidi, Innovative Party Planners LLC
  Owings Mills, MD
  www.zozzieandheidi.com

- *Carrie Katz*
  Creative Parties by Carrie
  Thousand Oaks, CA

- *Bruce Keslar*
  National Director,
  National Association of Mobile Entertainers
  Willow Grove, PA

- *Micah LaNasa*
  Emerald Bay Events
  www.emeraldbayevents.com

- *Paula Lundgren*
  Brainstorm Creative Business Services
  Saco, ME
  www.brainstormbiz.biz

- *Bernardo Puccio and Orin Kennedy*
  Puccio Designs, Inc.
  Los Angeles, CA

- *Carol Rejcek*
  Garden Gate
  Ennis, TX

- *Traci Romano*
  The Romano Group Event Planning + Design
  Fairfield, CT
  www.theromanogroup.net

- *Jennifer R. Rosciti*
  Dolce Event Productions
  Scituate, RI

- *Anne Spinelli*
  Party Characters
  Cumberland, RI
  www.partypop.com/Vendors/4076154.htm

- *Christine Stieber*
  The Perfect Day
  Fullerton, CA
  www.the-perfect-day.com

- *Myra Taylor*
  Special event planning
  Culver City, CA

- *Connie Thayer*
  Party Perfect
  Bellevue, WA

- *Betsie Trammel*
  P3 Professional Party Planners
  Indianapolis, IN

- *Eric Welch*
  Amazing Parties
  Tarzana, CA
  www.kiddcola.com

- *Lynn Wheatley*
  Lasting Impressions
  Tulsa, OK
  www.lastingimpressionsoftulsa.com

- *Bobbie Yarrusso*
  Creative Event Designs By Bobbie
  Wilmington, DE

1. Introduction

Congratulations on your decision to become a professional party planner. Everyone knows there's nothing better than being at a lively party where people are laughing and having a great time. As a party planner, you'll not only be immersed in a festive atmosphere, you'll also get the credit for every event that's a smash success.

Chances are that if you are considering pursuing party planning as a career, there's a reason for it. Do you have a love of bringing people together? Do you throw a great party? Party planners often say that they got the idea to make a career of party planning from the encouragement of others, who told them they had a talent for it.

Maybe you are the "go-to" person for office events like retirement parties or baby showers. People know that you have creative ideas, and are organized enough to handle all the details of planning a party (in addition to keeping up with your day job).

The personal satisfaction of being a party planner is enough to entice many people to pursue this career, but party planning can also be financially rewarding. Some party planners reach income levels of more than six figures, and have several employees on staff.

Just think of Debi Lilly of A Perfect Event, who put together Oprah's 50th birthday bash, or Mary Micucci of Along Came Mary Productions, who organizes star-studded Hollywood award show events every year. Lifestyle and event expert David Tutera transformed his skills for party planning into a popular book and TV show.

Whatever drew you to this career, it's time to take the leap from party expert to party professional, and get paid to use your talents. With the information in this book, your flair for knowing just the right look and music for every occasion, and your natural ability to organize anything down to the finest details, you're well on your way to becoming the toast of the town as a successful party planner.

1.1 Party Planning as a Profession

Party planning is an exciting way to make a living, and the future looks bright. Much of the baby boomer generation has acquired wealth in their pre-retirement years, but a lack of personal time has been the price. Hiring someone to plan a party for an occasion is considered a reasonable and necessary expense for these busy people.

We have witnessed the relatively recent explosion of magazines, TV shows and channels, and other popular media devoted to dining, decorating and entertaining in style. It has become expected that we can do it all with the flair of a Martha Stewart, but not everyone has that creative talent. That's where you as the party planner come in — to make the rest of us look good!

Also, the corporate party is currently seen as a great way to reward employees, and it's also a decent tax write-off for businesses. Those working as party planners are riding a wave of profitability brought on by this consumer willingness to spend on parties and party professionals. And it doesn't look as though the party atmosphere is going away anytime soon. Intrigued? Let's take a closer look at what the job entails.

1.1.1 What a Party Planner Does

Party planners organize and help execute social events. They meet with clients who are planning to host an event, and help them decide on a theme and set a budget. They purchase or make supplies on behalf of the client, meet and contract with venues and vendors, and arrange all the details that will be key to the event's success.

Some party planners make invitations and decorations themselves, or may purchase them at a discount from vendors. They set everything up in advance, and then are usually on hand to supervise the event and other service providers such as caterers from start to finish. They often coordinate the clean-up as well.

Party planners sell peace of mind to their clients. Instead of bustling around worrying about whether the punch is running low and when the band is going to show up, when they have hired a party planner the host can simply socialize and enjoy their party.

Vendors who are involved in professionally planned parties typically make their agreements with the planner, not directly with the client or venue. The planner is the one who has the authority and responsibility of carrying out the client's wishes.

Party planners are usually self-employed, and most work from a home office. Party planners are responsible for all the usual tasks associated with running a small business, such as paying bills, banking, and filing paperwork.

Most party planners also spend a good amount of their time seeking out new clients, especially when they are first starting their business. They may volunteer their time and expertise to get increased exposure, or dream up creative ads to place in magazines and local papers. And of course, networking with potential venues and vendors is a big part of the job.

Types of Planning Services

Although some people might refer to party planners as event planners, party planners have a specialty that sets them apart. Whereas an event planner may organize meetings and corporate seminars, party planners primarily only work on gatherings and events in which the primary focus is to socialize, celebrate and have fun.

So essentially, party planners are event planners who specialize in so-cial events. Other event planners with different specialties may call themselves meeting planners, destination management consultants, or wedding planners.

While the consequence of planning what is called an event and what is called a party is often much the same, most planners hold a distinction between the two.

"Event," explains Orin Kennedy of Puccio Designs, "means large — several hundred guests, like at a wedding, or something more corporate or charitable in nature, whereas a party could be anything from a dinner for 12 to a birthday or cocktail reception for 100 or more."

As you'll see, different party planners provide different levels of service, or may specialize in certain aspects of the party, such as entertainment. A party planner who provides full service will handle every detail of the party and attend it as well. They are responsible for hiring all of the vendors that may be needed like DJs and caterers, and will also coordinate their efforts. The party planner who provides partial services may be able to refer clients to their preferred vendors, but is usually not responsible for any aspect of the party beyond their agreed-upon contributions, such as decorating or planning a theme.

Party planner Bernard Puccio distinguishes between partial and complete planning with reference to whatever control the host of a party wants to retain. "Partial planning," he says, "might [only] involve those elements that the host will not be handling personally. We usually do it all, from the invitations to the cleanup. We are a complete [service] company."

Who Becomes a Party Planner?

Party planning is an attractive career for people who are creative, crafty, and who love meeting people and socializing. They usually like to entertain in their own homes, and are known for being warm and wonderful hosts. They are strong-willed, and good at getting what they want from (while maintaining good relationships with) people they work with.

Great party planners have a knack for coming up with unique ideas. They can see the potential for party décor and supplies in everyday items, and the potential for a great venue in an unremarkable place.

They know that a great party does not need to cost their clients a fortune.

A number of planners have started out in the party service business as caterers, DJs, or florists. They gradually expanded the scope of services that they offered so that they became planners who also provide catering or other services for the parties they plan.

In the case of Bernardo Puccio and his partner Orin Kennedy, their Los Angeles-based interior-design business evolved naturally into party and event planning. "The two [services] are so alike in the work process," Kennedy says. "Most of our party planning clients originate from our interior design clientele or are recommended by someone who's been a guest at one of our events."

With a Hollywood and Beverly Hills clientele, the Puccio design firm's mission evolved and enlarged to encompass entertainment and fundraising needs of a rich, famous, and satisfied client base. The expansion was organic because of the service orientation of entertainment planning and interior design.

1.1.2 Types of Parties

As a party planner, your clients will come to you with a broad range of party needs. Here are some of the types of events that party planners organize. As you read the list, think about what most interests you — that could become your specialty when you start up your business.

Private Parties

People throw events of all kinds for themselves, friends, and family, to mark milestones or celebrate holidays. You may have hosted or attended many of the following:

- Anniversaries

- Bar/bat mitzvahs

- Birthdays

- Bon voyage parties

- Children's parties

- Class reunions
- Dinner parties
- Engagement parties
- First communion/Confirmation parties
- Graduation parties
- Holiday parties
- Open-house parties
- Wedding showers

All of these and more may require the services of a party planner. The more guests the host wants to invite, the more likely it is that planning services will be requested.

Some individuals who use party planners are accustomed to entertaining and are prepared to use planners either to execute their ideas precisely or to support them with "idea help" in limited ways. "We deal with people who throw parties all the time," says Micah LaNasa, marketing director for Emerald Bay Events, a Seattle-area full-service planning firm. "They know what they want, but may need help going to the next level."

Like many other party planners, Emerald also deals with what LaNasa describes as "people who have never thrown a party in their lives." You may have to handhold insecure clients through the process as it goes along, either tempering or accommodating new requests, as needed.

Corporate Parties

When you think about planning parties your first thought may be of private events. However, there is a need for party planners in the corporate world as well. Corporate events may require you to do more work, but they also generally pay more. Businesses may use planners to coordinate social events such as:

- Annual holiday parties
- Company picnics or family days
- Corporate anniversaries

- Product launches
- Open houses
- Celebrating business success
- Employee social events
- Awards banquets
- Luncheons

Planning corporate events often requires more lead-up time, and the decision-making process may be more complex. Frequently you will report to more than one person, and possibly a committee of involved individuals. Ideally, you want to identify one main decision-maker to work with — many businesses have on staff a person or persons who may be familiar with party-planning territory.

Some corporations have rather elaborate approval processes for every stage of every project. According to planner Micah LaNasa, there is no guarantee of getting one central point of contact with corporate clients. "We've had an army of five or six people come in, so that we made a presentation to a committee," he explains.

Fundraising Parties

Planning parties for nonprofit organizations entails many of the same issues as is the case for the corporate market, plus a few unique ones. Some nonprofits require the input of board members in making decisions. Orin Kennedy of Puccio Designs in Los Angeles cites "the complexities of reporting to committees" when dealing with parties and events for nonprofits.

Add to this the issue of financial constraints. Nonprofits that throw big parties frequently do so for the purpose of raising funds, not spending them. You'll need to be creative in seeking services on a budget, and may even be asked to donate your time as well. While this might seem like a strange idea, there are extensive networking opportunities that make working with nonprofits (at least some of the time) attractive to party planners.

Your contacts with those who may be involved in a community-service organization, as well as the wealthy people who donate might wish to turn to you in the future for their entertainment-planning needs. You can also use nonprofit events to build your portfolio and awareness of your services.

1.1.3   Benefits of this Career

Party planning is an exciting, fun and creative career that offers the flexibility of working from home, but without the isolation that sometimes comes with home-based businesses. This is because you're always meeting new people, visiting new places and, yes, going to parties.

We've already touched on what a growing and potentially lucrative market the party planning industry is right now. But the benefits of this career don't end here. Here's a short but impressive list of some of the benefits enjoyed by party planners.

Enjoyable Work

In what profession other than party planning can you visit the ballroom of a castle in the morning, taste the salmon and champagne to be served at an upcoming event in the afternoon, and attend an elegant soirée that evening? Few others can claim that they have this much fun in a lifetime, let alone a day.

And the reason is clear: it's a profession built around creating fun, so you're bound to get in the way of the revelry from time to time. Just think of picking out decorations for a 50th anniversary party, or watching a child's face light up when a life-sized Dora the Explorer walks through the door. It can become difficult to differentiate between work and play in this career.

Being Creative

Many creative people are drawn to party planning, and it doesn't disappoint. Decorating venues, making your own centerpieces, setting elegant tables, and crafting stylish invitations are just a few of the creative outlets for party planners. The entire industry is one in which you are constantly being creatively challenged, and consistently working with other creative people.

More than this, the options for the types of party services that you provide are wide open. You can focus on throwing children's or adult parties, wedding-related parties or corporate affairs, or make the focus of your parties centered around wonderfully catered meals. The choice is yours.

Working from Home

Many people dream of working from home, setting their own hours, and being their own boss. The low start-up cost and lack of need for equipment and space make party planning perfect as a home-based business. In fact, few in the industry operate anywhere other than from home. Other than set times for parties, this career offers the flexibility of setting your own hours and schedule.

Unlimited Income Potential

The trend of hiring party planners to throw all types of parties has created an industry in which income potential is only limited by the drive and imagination of the individual.

Corporate parties can earn party planners thousands of dollars for a single event. Even a small start-up party business throwing birthday, graduation and anniversary parties will earn the planner at least $25 to $30 an hour, and many charge much more. And the opportunity to be earning six figures as the planner for high-end or celebrity events exists for those who make it to the top.

You Can Start Right Now

Party planners do not require a degree in "festivity studies" (okay, we made that up!) or any special certification or licensing to get started. From the first day you arrange to plan a get-together for a friend or relative, you can start calling yourself a party planner.

Additionally, this is the kind of business you can start with a few hundred dollars in your pocket. You don't need many supplies since you are selling "yourself" and your great party ideas.

1.2 Inside This Guide

This book is a guide to getting started in the thrilling world of party planning. It provides industry information on everything from the skills you'll need, to finding the right venues for your parties. Here's a first glance at what you'll find in the chapters ahead.

Chapter 2 takes a step-by-step look at the logistics of planning a party for a client. It covers the initial meeting, selecting a location, designing the creative elements such as theme and décor, getting yourself and your events organized, and what your role is once the first guests arrive.

Chapter 3 helps you prepare for your career as a party planner by identifying the skills that you need to succeed, and providing you with the tools and resources for enhancing these skills. It also tells how to gain valuable experience through training and volunteer experience.

Chapter 4 offers concrete advice on starting your own party planning business. It also looks at preparing a business plan and a start-up budget, as well as some of the legal matters associated with doing business, and those unique to party planning.

Chapter 5 looks at the secrets of running a successful party planning business, starting with setting up your office, the equipment you'll need, and how to hire staff or contractors. The importance of your relationship with vendors, and how to enhance this relationship, is covered in detail. Finally, the all-important issue of what and how to charge your clients is explained in this section.

Chapter 6 provides tips on finding those clients out there who want to throw a party. Marketing strategies such as brochures, websites and advertising are compared and contrasted. Alternative ways for your party planning business to get the attention that it needs are also explored.

Throughout the book are insights and tips from more than 20 successful party planners and party industry experts, as well as checklists and forms you can adapt and use for your own business. So if you're ready, let's get this party started!

2. How to Plan a Party

You've probably planned a bash or two in your lifetime, especially if you're reading this book. Planning parties for clients will follow many of the steps you used to plan your own parties, but will have the added component of your client's input.

For example, you might be thinking that fireworks at midnight would be perfect, but since your client's terrier is terrified of loud noises, you're back to the drawing board. In some ways you are like a commissioned artist or architect. You are expected to make the client's "napkin sketches" become the realization of their dreams. No pressure!

Most people don't put a ton of thought into the steps of planning a party —they just go ahead and do it, with mixed results. Maybe the punch was a flop (way too boozy!) or maybe guests left because the music was too loud, or nonexistent.

The point of hiring a planner is so that no detail is missed. For this reason, we're going to break down the components of planning a party in this chapter, to turn you into the ultimate party planning expert that your clients will brag about long after the dancing stops and the guests have gone home.

2.1 Meet with Clients

The phone rings, and it's someone calling about your party planning services. You will get a few details over the phone about what they have in mind, and then ask the client what would be a good time for you to meet up so you can assess their needs.

This initial meeting is an important part of the service you provide. Your goal is not necessarily to get the client to sign a contract on the spot, but to get them interested enough in what you can do to get the go-ahead to prepare a proposal. In the proposal you will outline your unique ideas for the party, as well as give concrete budget numbers for the client that include your fees.

In this section we'll take a look at the information you will gather in your initial meeting, and what to put in a budget and proposal. Later in the guide we'll explain how to contact vendors, how to set your fees, and what to put in your contract.

Of course it's possible that someone will enlist you to work with them without asking to see a breakdown of what the party will cost them, or hear how you will make the event special. However, the vast majority of clients will want you to "sell them" a party package they can't resist. Here's how to do just that.

2.1.1 Why Have a Meeting?

At your first meeting with a client you'll gather information on the kind of party that is being planned, and get a big-picture idea of the guest list and concept. With repeat clients you might be able to get these details by phone or fax, but with new clients you definitely want to have an in-person meeting.

Especially if they have never worked with a party planner, your prospective client may have common hesitations such as:

- "Can I afford a party planner? I'm already spending so much on the party!"

- "What exactly does a party planner do?"

- "What if I don't like your party ideas?"

- "Maybe there is another party planner who could do a better job..."

In the initial meeting, you are going to set these fears to rest. You want your client to walk out the door afterwards thinking about what great value you provide, how creative your ideas are, how you nearly seem to read their mind, and that you are certainly the best planner to do the job. And that's a lot easier to do face to face.

> **TIP:** Take advantage of laptops and PowerPoint software to develop a presentation of what you can do for a client, including photos of parties you have worked on in the past. You can take a PowerPoint training course at almost any community college.

Some clients may resist a meeting, or push you for prices over the phone. By definition, people who hire party planners are busy and don't like to waste their precious time. You want to avoid giving a dollar-figure, though, or you may scare them away. You can say something like:

> "It depends on your party budget and the scope of the services you want, but I can usually save you money on supplies with my preferred vendors. Let's take an hour to sit down together so I can figure out what you need, and fully explain my services."

If you want to be better prepared for your initial meeting, you can ask your client to fill out and fax you a *New Client Inquiry* similar to the one on the next page, reprinted with permission. You will be better prepared to move ahead quickly with planning the party after some introductory input from your client.

2.1.2   The Information You Need

Greet the potential client with a warm smile and a firm (not crippling) handshake. Express a genuine interest in making their party a success.

Sample New Client Inquiry

NEW CLIENT INQUIRY

Today's Date: _____ Appt. Date/Time: _____

Name: _____ Guest of Honor: _____

Home Phone: _____ Work Phone: _____

Address: _____ E-mail: _____

_____ Fax and/or Cell: _____

Best place/time to reach: _____

____ Bar/Bat Mitzvah ___Birthday ___Anniversary ___Wedding ___Corporate

Event Date: _____ Time: _____

Location: _____ Caterer: _____

Theme: _____ Number of Guests: _____

How did you hear about us? _____

Additional information: _____

_____

_____

_____

_____

_____

_____

_____

Follow Up: _____

Form is copyrighted and appears courtesy of Innovative Party Planners, LLC

After you have introduced yourself to the client, you'll start to ask questions about the party they have in mind.

Be delighted to help them with their event, and listen carefully as they describe what they want. You will assess the following details with your client:

- The type of party

- A preferred date, time and venue

- The guest list

- The party elements

After you have identified what the client wants, then you can explain to them what services you offer, and how you can meet their needs. Information from the first meeting may change as the event shapes up, but your purpose is to start building a proposal on the basic facts of the event.

Type of Party

The first thing to assess with your prospective client is why the party is being held. Here we are not talking about themes like luaus or the 1980s, but about the reason for getting together. If you know what the goals of a party are, you are in a better position to design the party plan with those specific goals in mind.

Some people give parties just for fun. Other parties are linked to anniversaries, birthdays, or holidays. Still other parties have fundraising as their main objective. Some possible party goals your client may have in mind are:

- To mark an occasion

- To celebrate an individual

- To celebrate a holiday

- To bring together diverse groups of friends

- To socialize and have fun

- To raise money or awareness

- To boost morale

- To celebrate nature

- To show off new homes or purchases

- Just because…

Sometimes the goals of a party may not be simple or straightforward. Think of the goals of a party sponsored by a nonprofit organization. While the purpose of the party might be advertised as "celebrating Christmas in the community," its objective could be to obtain contributions from donors for the local soup kitchen. You as the party planner will need to balance both goals effectively.

"Learn as much as you can about the client, and what the obvious motivation is for the event as well as any underlying motivations. I like to ask my clients about the best event they have attended (and the worst)," explains Kathleen Kellner of Eventful Productions. "I need to make sure that my ideas and expectations for the event are the same as the stakeholders, and that they will be happy with the results," she affirms.

Date, Time and Venue

You should speak with the client about a date and time they have in mind for their party, as well as where they were thinking about holding it. They may have something specific in mind, or they may be looking to you for input and creative ideas. Some events such as birthday parties are going to have to take place within a specific window of time, but other events such as holiday season parties may offer more flexibility when it comes to choosing a date.

Date and time need to be chosen with the nature of the event in mind. If the party is supposed to be outdoors, check with the weather office for average temperatures and daylight hours at that time of year, and advise your client if they are appropriate. Sometimes even two weeks can make all the difference.

Check that the date doesn't conflict with events the client's guests might not want to miss, such as the Super Bowl or season premiere of a popular TV show (unless that's the party's purpose and theme)!

TIP: Avoid opening a day planning book in front of the client if your book is brand new or makes it appear you have nothing going on.

Quite simply, sometimes a date and time are not going to be available to a client at a specific venue. That's why you need to prepare your client to identify alternate dates and venues in your initial interview.

If you know your local venues well, you may be able to convince the client to use another facility that is equally nice or better, or offers some other benefit such as a reduced price. Or you may be able to explain the advantages of choosing a different date. This guide will cover the pros and cons of different venues in more detail in section 2.2.

If your client is flexible on the date, then they can be more particular about the venue. If your client is flexible on the venue, then they can be choosier about the date. If your client is adamant about both date and venue — then you may run into a challenge!

Lead time, or the amount of time between the plan and the party, is also important. For certain key elements such as the venue and caterer, you may need to begin planning up to six months in advance of an event. This is especially true when the venue is popular, the guest list is extensive, or it's a busy time of year.

Be cautious about taking rush jobs at busy times if you're new to the business and your vendor relations are not yet well established. If you are unable to pull a party off and it ends up a disaster, your reputation could be ruined. Ask a client for 48 hours to contact vendors on their availability before you commit to something risky. If it looks iffy, it may be wise to pass on the job.

By working out a rough timeline of tasks, you can establish if there is enough lead time to plan the party in the time your client has in mind. (Not sure where to start? No worries — we'll show you how to prepare a timeline in section 2.4.1.)

Guest List

Parties are most often private events that have exclusive and specific guest lists. You should get a preliminary idea of the number and type of guests at your initial meeting with the client. Your client should have a guest list prepared, or at least an idea of how many people are likely to be invited or attend.

Alternately, sometimes the client will have a budget and concept to work with, and will base a guest list on that. For example, say the planners for the office Christmas party have a budget of $5,000 to work with, and 100 employees. If you can plan a party that cost approximately $25 per guest (e.g. appetizers and wine), they can invite spouses for a guest list of 200, but if their concept costs more like $50 per guest (e.g. full-course dinner and drinks), then it will be employees only, and the guest list is back to 100.

In addition to nailing down an approximate number of guests, ask about the average age of attendees, and what ratio of men, women and children are expected to attend. This will have a bearing on the creative elements of your party, such as décor, theme, and food and drink selection.

You can let your client know about guest-list services you may offer, such as designing and printing invitations, preparing labels, or receiving RSVPs. Your client may be comfortable handling these things, or they may welcome your services in those areas.

Some of these tasks may be a part of your "standard service," while others may come with an additional cost to the client. Party planning company Puccio Designs told us they most definitely insist on handling the invitation for every party they coordinate, since it is the first impression that people have of the occasion. You may wish to set a similar policy for your business, especially if your work is more high-end.

Keep in mind that if you offer these services, there will be more work involved for you. However, the benefit is that offering some of these add-on services might be the special "something" that sets you above and beyond other planners. Section 2.3.2 of this guide will explain more about planning guest lists and designing invitations for parties.

Creative Elements

The client may have specific creative elements they want to include in the party, which you can jot down to work with. For example, if they are planning a Western-themed party, they may be envisioning hay bales to sit on, a live country band, and beans and beef brisket served buffet style.

Start by asking your client for a general description of the party atmosphere. Will it be classy? Traditional? Silly? Outrageous? Trendy? Kitschy? Formal? Intellectual? Adjectives such as these are a great help to you a party planner, since they will direct the creative elements you choose.

Next, ask the client if they have anything specific in mind for each of the following creative elements. If not, reassure them that you will "wow" them with some great options in your proposal:

- Theme

- Invitations

- Food

- Drink

- Music

- Entertainment

- Décor

- Games and activities

- Gift bags

You can jot down your own notes, or fill out a form like the one on the next few pages as you speak with your client. When you have all the information you think you need, thank the client and let them know you will get in touch with your vendors, and get back to them with a creative, complete proposal as soon as your schedule allows.

Most party planners take two to three business days to work on a proposal, or less time if possible. "The biggest challenge can be getting quotes from suppliers so I do try to ensure that I have up to date sales packages from venues and other suppliers to quote from," Kathleen Kellner told us.

Sample Initial Client Interview

Basic Information

Today's Date: _____

Party Planner's Name: _____

Name of Event/Party (If applicable): _____

Date of Event/Party: _____

Approx. Start Time: _____

Approx. End Time: _____

Alternate Date #1: _____

Alternate Date #2: _____

Name of Host: _____

Name of Event Contact: _____

Title of Event Contact: _____

Name of Organization: _____

Address: _____

Phone: _____

Cell Phone: _____

Fax: _____

Email: _____

Best Times to Reach: _____

Type of Party (check all that apply):

❑ Anniversary	❑ Dining	❑ Motivational
❑ Awards	❑ Dining and dancing	❑ Product demonstration
❑ Bar mitzvah/ Bat mitzvah	❑ Election	❑ Promotion
❑ Birthday	❑ Graduation	❑ Reception
❑ Bon voyage	❑ Holiday	❑ Retirement
❑ Charity event	❑ Homecoming	❑ Other:
❑ Cocktail	❑ Memorial	_____

Party Purpose

What are the purposes and objectives of this party?

_____

_____

_____

What is the theme? _____

Alternates? _____

Who is the guest or guests of honor? _____

Their age and gender? _____

Other pertinent information?

_____

_____

_____

Is this party going to be a surprise? _____

Guest Profile

Approx. number of guests to invite: _____

Approx. number expected to attend: _____

Approx. ratio of male to female guests: _____

Check one: ❏ Adults only
               ❏ Children only
               ❏ Adults and children

Special needs guests?   ❏ Yes   ❏ No

Details:

_____

_____

_____

Public Figures/Celebrities? ❑ Yes ❑ No

Details:

_____

_____

Childcare services required:

_____

_____

Other guest-related information:

_____

_____

Venue Profile

Check one: ❑ Indoor ❑ Indoor/Outdoor

              ❑ Outdoor ❑ Venue Still to be Determined

Check one: ❑ Hotel ❑ Private Home

              ❑ Restaurant ❑ Other: _____

Preferred venue: _____

Alternate venue: _____

Importance of this item on 1–10 scale: _____

Food and Beverage

Do you need the party planner to locate a caterer? ❑ Yes ❑ No

Preferred caterer: _____

Meal details:

_____

_____

Bar service? ❏ Yes ❏ No

Details:

_____

_____

Special dietary concerns:

_____

_____

Other food and beverage information:

_____

_____

Importance of this item on 1–10 scale: _____

Invitations:

_____

_____

_____

Importance of this item on 1–10 scale: _____

Music:

_____

_____

_____

Importance of this item on 1–10 scale: _____

Entertainment:

_____

_____

Importance of this item on 1–10 scale: _____

Décor:

_____

_____

Importance of this item on 1–10 scale: _____

Games and Activities:

_____

_____

Importance of this item on 1–10 scale: _____

Gift Bags:

_____

_____

Importance of this item on 1–10 scale: _____

Other Information/Notes:

_____

_____

_____

When will we meet next to discuss this party?

Date: _____   Time: _____

2.1.3 Budgeting

When you have all the details in place, it's time to start getting an idea of how much a party is going to cost your client. Your client will have given you an amount they want to spend, and now it's time to make sure that their ideas match their imagination.

When your client gives you a budget number in your initial meeting, make sure that you ask them about what percentages they want to allot to different party elements. What do they want to spend the most on? Where would they prefer to economize? Great food may be a priority, but the client could live without the live band. Rate the importance of each element to the client on a scale of 1 – 10.

Budgets need to be comprehensive, so there are relatively few surprises. The best way to be prepared to do a party budget is to have met with suppliers and service providers in advance, but it's likely you'll need to make a few phone calls anyway. You'll read all about working with vendors in section 5.3.

Once you have been in business for a while you may be comfortable giving clients an approximate budget on the spot (i.e., before you call around for pricing). Don't do this unless you are very sure of your estimate, though.

If the client knows exactly what they want, your budget numbers will be more accurate. If they are vague on big aspects like a venue, you can prepare more than one budget with different aspects combined. For example, venue A plus caterer A, venue B plus caterer A, etc. Your client's biggest costs are likely to be the venue rental, food and drink, and sometimes entertainment. You will also account for equipment, decorating, and any other items that are necessary to pull the event together, from a smoke machine to a balloon release.

Remember, the more details you account for in budget planning, the better. One of the most common mistakes people make when they plan their own parties is not accounting for unexpected costs.

Sure, a bag of ice doesn't cost much, but how many does it take to fill the antique bathtub your client wants to stock with beer at their summer barbeque? And then how many replacement bags will they need as it melts in the blazing sun? As a party planner, your "edge" is that you are an expert on these details.

It's also a good idea to have quotes from back-up service providers or suppliers in case a client balks at a certain suggestion. For example, if their cousin got married at the place you had in mind and they had a terrible experience there, you're not likely to change their mind.

When you present the budget to your client, don't forget to factor your own fees in as well. You will learn all about setting your fees in section 5.4 of this guide. You can also ask the client to set aside a small emergency fund (5 to 10 percent of the total budget) for unexpected expenses.

We have included a *Sample Event Budget Checklist* later in this section for you to use as a guide. You'll notice it's pretty comprehensive, since parties can vary in the kinds of expenses involved. You may not have to handle every single item on that form, but it's best to give each some consideration in the planning stages. You may also want to prepare a simplified document that you can share with clients, so they don't get overwhelmed.

If you just want to get some general, approximate costs for party elements, there is an online budget calculator at the PartyPop website. You can also use this to practice preparing budgets before you need to get real with a client. The PartyPop Budget Calculator can be found at **www.partypop.com/budget_calculator.htm**.

If you're not a pen and paper/calculator kind of person, there is party planning software that will allow to you quickly create budgets, construct a proposal, and link them to to-do lists. They will also let you manage your payroll if you have one, and make sure vendors get paid on time. Although they are mainly designed for the host to use for their own party, you may find them useful if numbers really make your head swim. We list a few examples in section 5.1.2.

Or you might want to use a spreadsheet and/or database program to computerize your own to-do lists and budgeting needs. A lot of spreadsheet programs include planning templates that can get you started.

Sample Event Budget Checklist

FOOD & BEVERAGE BUDGET

Item	Provided By	Approx. Cost
Appetizers		
Entrée		
Dessert		
Caterer's fee		
Wine		
Beer		
Other alcohol		
Bar supplies		
Bartender		
Wait Service Staff		
Table/chair rental		
Linen/china		
Flatware/glassware		
Delivery		
Tips		
Taxes		
Other		
Food & Beverage Subtotal:		

ENTERTAINMENT BUDGET

Item	Provided By	Approx. Cost
DJ		
Emcee		
Musicians		
CDs		
Entertainers		
Celebrity guests		
Specialty lights		
TV/Film screening		
Games		
Animal wrangler		
Other		
Entertainment Subtotal:		

DÉCOR BUDGET

Item	Provided By	Approx. Cost
Designer Fee		
Lighting		
Flowers		
Table décor		
Balloons		
Candles		
Gift bags		
Gift bag items		
Other		
Décor Subtotal:		

AUDIOVISUAL BUDGET		
Item	Provided By	Approx. Cost
Setup fee		
Bullhorn		
Camera		
DVD player		
Extension cords		
Handheld microphone		
Karaoke setup		
Laptop		
Laser pointer		
Lectern/podium		
Overhead projector		
Projection screen		
Projector table		
Slide projector		
Sound system		
Tripod		
VCR		
Video camera		
Walkie talkie		
Other		
	AV Subtotal:	

PRINTING BUDGET		
Item	**Provided By**	**Approx. Cost**
Auction tickets		
Awards		
Dining menu		
Display card		
Door prize tickets		
ID badge		
Invitation		
Mailing stationery		
Mailing list		
Maps		
Napkins, coasters		
Photocopies		
Place cards		
Program		
Response card		
Seating plan		
Directional signs		
Thank-you notes		
Tickets		
Clerical support fee		
Other		
Printing Subtotal:		

VENUE BUDGET

Item	Provided By	Approx. Cost
Facilities rental fee		
Plating or corking fee		
Guest rooms		
Coat check service		
Furniture rental		
Table skirts		
Bleachers or risers		
Crowd control ropes		
Canopy		
Tent		
Heaters		
Other		
Venue Subtotal:		

LOGISTICS BUDGET

Item	Provided By	Approx. Cost
On site child care		
Valet service		
Security		
Setup/strike crew		
Casual labor		
Cleanup supplies		
Portable restrooms		
Trash service		
Generator/power source		
Other		
Logistics Subtotal:		

PUBLICITY BUDGET		
Item	Provided By	Approx. Cost
Direct mail ads		
Flyers		
Internet ads		
Magazine ads		
Newspapers ads		
Radio ads		
Signage		
TV ads		
Press kit		
Photography		
Videography		
Other		
Publicity Subtotal:		

G&A EXPENSES		
Item	Provided By	Approx. Cost
Accounting		
Legal		
Insurance		
Permits		
Office supplies		
Parking		
Courier		
Postage		
Telephone		
Vehicle/mileage		
Other		
G&A Expenses Subtotal:		

SOURCES OF INCOME	
Item	**Estimated Income**
Auction/silent auction	
Sponsors	
Donations	
Door prize tickets	
Gift baskets	
Photography	
Product sales	
Program advertising	
Ticket sales	
Other	
Income Subtotal:	

BUDGET TOTALS	
Item	**Approx. Cost**
Food & Beverage	
Entertainment	
Audiovisual	
Printing	
Décor	
Venue	
Logistics	
Publicity & Promotion	
G&A Expenses	
Subtotal 1:	
Emergency Fund (5-10 percent of subtotal 1)	
Party Planner Fee (___% of subtotal 1)	
Subtotal 2:	
Minus Event Income	
Total Budget for Event:	

Budgeting gets easier the longer you are in business, since you will have past numbers to look back on. Keep copies of invoices or estimates from service providers (even if you don't use them) and file them away, and you'll eventually have a great budgeting resource at your fingertips.

2.1.4   Presenting a Proposal

When you've got your budget and concept together, it's time to meet with your client and present a proposal. If there is an organization committee, you may be asked to make a formal presentation of your proposal to the group.

Many planners charge a nonrefundable deposit ($100 to $200) to create a proposal, and apply that charge against their fee if the client goes ahead with the party. This makes sure that you get paid even if the client changes their mind about hosting a get-together.

You probably don't want client prospects who balk at paying that fee when they anticipate spending several thousand dollars on a fancy bash. Attaching a fee to a proposal declares that your time and ideas have value.

> **TIP:**   If you are responding to an RFP (Request For Proposal) to organize an event for a business or organization, you normally would not get paid for preparing the proposal. However, the lucrative nature of these kinds of jobs makes taking the risk of not getting paid one that may be worth your while.

In addition to going over the client's concept of the party and the general manner in which you will plan it, as well as a timeline for getting things done, the proposal should lay out the terms of payment. You can use a letter of agreement format, or a formal contract. (You will see samples of these typical agreements later in section 4.4, which covers legal matters.)

Bring your materials in a business-like tote, folder or briefcase. Leather is generally good; a handsome vinyl may suffice. An attractive canvas tote may work as well for casual meetings.

Closing The Sale

If the idea of closing the sale is intimidating, you're not alone. Even for seasoned salespeople, getting to yes is the hardest. Countering a potential client's objections is easier if you have thought of the answers ahead of time.

The biggest misconception about hiring a party planner is that it's not affordable. Planner Teresa Choate has an answer for this roadblock to making the sale. "Yes, you can afford it! Come and meet with me and I'll explain it to you," she tells customers. She then goes through a checklist of party expenses, and areas where she can save them money and heartache by handling it or getting her professional discounts.

If everything about the meeting has gone well, you feel like the potential client loves what you have to say and would be the perfect candidate to become a client, smile and confidently ask for the chance to do their party contract.

There are many ways to close a sale. Read any book on selling to get ideas, or talk to anyone you know who does sales in any field and ask them how they do it. You will develop your own unique way to close the deal. A good close can also be used on the phone, if you made arrangements to get back to the client with a proposal. Here are some sample closing statements:

- "Ms. Doskill, I think we have a clear understanding of what will make your party really special. (Briefly go over the pertinent details.) I would love to work with you on this. Can I plan your party?"

- "So, an Elvis-themed party honoring your wife on her 65th birthday, with 65 guests, an Elvis impersonator and a Graceland-themed menu. Wonderful! Mr. Holton, it sounds like we agree on what it takes to make this party very memorable for you and your guests. I'd like to plan this for you. May I draft up a contract and bring it by your office this afternoon for your signature?"

- "Cindy, I think this party will be wonderful, and I love the pirate theme. Let's plan it! Shall I draft up a straightforward agreement?"

You have made the preliminary agreement to plan the party. Thank the client for his business and stress that you are excited about planning the party. Remind them of the next step, shake hands and go get working!

- "Ginny, thanks very much for the opportunity to plan your party. It is going to be great! I'll get that contract over to you this afternoon, and have those estimates for you by Friday."

Getting a Deposit

Once you have a formal agreement in place, it's time to start planning. It is common for party planners to ask their client for 50 percent of the party budget up front, so that you can put down deposits and pay for supplies. "Once I have confirmed a client I generally ask for a 50 percent deposit for the total event cost. This will cover any deposits to caterers, venues and other suppliers. I then pay most suppliers rather than the client paying the supplier direct," confirms Kathleen Kellner.

2.2 Select a Location

If you have done your homework, you should have accumulated details on possible venues for a party that your client can look over. We'll explain how to meet with vendors and assess venues in section 5.3.4 of this guide. For now, we'll take a look at some of the pros and cons of hosting at home versus a remote location, and the details your client will want to consider.

2.2.1   Hosting at a Private Home

For small get-togethers, dinner parties, and cocktail parties, hosting a party at home may be the best option. Hosting at home may also be appropriate if the home is part of the reason for the party — a house-warming, for example. Hosting from home is popular because it is convenient to decorate, does not cost anything to rent, comes complete with furniture and supplies, and is familiar and comfortable to the host.

If your client wants to host a party at their home, make sure you explain to them the drawbacks too. Let them know that their home could be damaged, their rugs stained, or their gardens trampled. They will have to "stay" until the last guest leaves, and they may need to hire service staff.

Additionally, they'll need to clean their home before and after the event, stock up on supplies like napkins and toilet paper, and may even need to rearrange furniture to create more space. If any of these details seems to bother your client a great deal, ask them if they would prefer to look at hosting at another site instead.

Be sure to take a realistic look at the logistics before you agree to plan a party at any private home. If your client wants to host at home and you are concerned about space, do a realistic and systematic assessment that takes into account bathroom use, parking, physical space, furniture, and safety.

Hosting 50 people in the ballroom of a big mansion with eight bathrooms on a five-acre estate is one thing; the same thing is not practical in a standard-sized home. Parking, kitchen, and bathroom facilities would be strained to the max, and service providers, not to mention guests, would be stumbling all over one another.

For a larger at-home party you will probably be hiring a valet parking service. "I always employ the best valet services in town that can be depended upon in any situation," explains planner Orin Kennedy, citing a parking disaster at a private party that he once attended as a guest. "The valets walked off the job, and the guests' cars were being towed."

When valets park cars on the public street, the residential infrastructure will be strained. In some cities you have to get a special permit to temporarily close one or more streets, and you might have to submit a written plan explaining the reason for your closure request.

> TIP: Puccio Designs' Orin Kennedy says it is "a considerate choice" to personally notify neighbors of a planned party in a neighborhood that is going to be affected by party-related parking and noise, even if no special permit is required.

2.2.2   Parties at a Public Venue

The advantages of hosting an event somewhere other than your client's home are obvious: they can usually accommodate bigger groups, your client does not have to clean up or arrange for service, food and drink are often part of the venue's service, and all the tables and chairs will be set up and ready to go.

Of course, a venue often comes with a price. While bars and restaurants may be happy to charge only the cost of food and drink plus gratuity, hotels and other businesses that sell "location" will require a fee to host the event.

Ideally, you should assemble venue information before you start planning any parties. That way you can examine the promotional material of these places and follow up with questions for their event people at a time when you're not being pushed by deadlines. Section 5.3.4 has a form you can fill out for each venue that has details that may be relevant to your client's party, such as the following:

- How many people they can accommodate
- If a private room is available
- Food and drink availability/menus
- Parking availability

The Joy of Outdoor Parties

Nothing says "party" like an outdoor event. Popular locations for outdoor parties include the beach, rooftop patios, backyards, campgrounds, parks, picnic areas, and ranches.

These locales are a little trickier to plan for. Weather becomes a concern, as do restrooms, power sources, sun protection, garbage disposal, safety, noise levels, bugs, keeping food and drink cold, and privacy. Even the weather leading up to the party may affect attendance (it rained all day; everything must be soaking wet!).

Outdoor locations can also put limits on serving alcohol particularly if they are public spaces. There are sometimes restrictions on numbers of guests at public parks, and fire bans in place that can put a damper on things if they come as a surprise. And you may have a required hour that things need to shut down for the night.

If your client is keen on hosting an outdoor party, you'll need to be extra-careful making sure all the logistics are workable. Visit the locale if you haven't before, and make notes about what amenities are available. It's not a bad idea to take pictures as well.

Have all your city permits in place (see below) and be aware of any restrictions. Not every outdoor venue will require it, but make reservations if necessary as well. Remind guests on the invite to dress for the weather, and to bring their outdoor needs. Of course, you can stock your production box (see section 5.1.2) with extras just in case.

Outdoor events leave a lot of room for creativity when it comes to decorating. You can use outdoor lighting such as tiki torches and strings of lights to create a romantic or intriguing setting, and unique canopies to offer protection from the elements and/or privacy for small groups. Be creative to help your host hold a remarkable event.

- Handicap access

- Dress code

- Closing time/last call

- When you can get in to decorate

- Rental cost

- Required deposit

- Cancellation policy

Talk to your client about whether any of these factors are a concern to them. You can use the details your client provides about their concept for a party to match a venue to the event. Get a few options together in case one is booked up, though.

Hotels, says Bernardo Puccio, are the "most obvious choice" for venues because they tend to have a full complement of food and beverage services and supplies in-house, as well as the ability to supply wait staff, bartenders, etc. Puccio says that after hotels, the best locations for parties (in order) tend to be nightclubs, restaurants, and special-request sites such as the beach. If you pick a less-trendy, out-of-the-way locale, you won't have any trouble booking it, and you may end up with more privacy in the long run.

Reserving a space generally requires a deposit amounting to at least half of the amount of rental (sometimes more) plus a cleaning deposit, security deposit, and possibly an insurance deposit. Cancellation without financial penalty may be possible three or four weeks in advance, but larger venues will probably charge a cancellation fee, and that fee will go up the closer to the scheduled event a cancellation comes in.

Your venue reservation might change if the number of guests increases — for example, if a charity gathering attracts more than the usual number of attendees. Plan for that from the time you first start dealing with the client, and raise the possibility with the venue manager up front.

2.2.3   Licenses and Permits

Do you need a license to party? You bet! Not every bash will require paperwork and fees, but many will. The rule of thumb is that the more conventional your party's location, the less likely you will need special permits for anything. The more unconventional the venue, the more likely you will need something special.

Permits usually come into the picture if you intend to host a party on public property. Very large gatherings that may involve extensive delivery-truck traffic may require moving or traffic permits of some kind. Be aware that you need to apply for these permits well in advance of the party date (i.e., not a few days before).

Where you make applications for special permits varies with the community, but expect to be in contact with city planning boards, zoning commissions, parks and recreation bureaus, fire departments, police departments, traffic-control bureaus, and alcohol-regulation agencies. There may be fees attached to reviews and inspections.

Here is a closer look at some of the licenses and permits that you may require before throwing a party.

Special Events License

Most regions require that a special events license be purchased when holding a party in a public space. The cost, if any, will depend on the type of party being thrown, the type of equipment being used (tents, barbeques, etc.), and the date of the party (weekend or holiday). These generally must be purchased approximately three weeks in advance of the party date. See your local licensing office for details.

Street Closing Permit

Street parties have been around as long as there have been streets. If a client asks you to arrange a street party for them, you will require a city permit that gives you and your client permission to close off the street for a specified amount of time. Again, this must be obtained well in advance of the date, and costs will vary. If alcohol is being served, this may require a special street permit or additional alcohol license.

Parks Permit

City parks have become hot spots for holding parties. To have a party in a park, a city-issued park permit is required. These are easily obtained and the cost, if any, is often minimal. However, these party spots fill up fast, particularly in the summer months, so be sure to book well in advance. Separate fire and cooking permits may also be needed.

Alcohol License

Unless you're having your client's party at a private home or licensed establishment, having alcoholic beverages will require an alcohol license. These licenses often come in different designations for different types of alcohol, such as one for beer and wine, and one that allows the sale or distribution of spirits as well. Licensing offices are very stringent about providing these, and may require that a criminal record check be performed for applicants.

Noise Ordinance

Most, if not all, regions have noise ordinances to restrict loud noise to certain hours of the day. Be sure to check with local officials about the noise laws in the area of your client's party venue.

Others

More rarely you may need to apply for one of the following:

- Barricade permit

- Dance permits

- Entertainment permits

- Fencing permits

- Film/photography permit

- Fire permit

- Hauling and moving permits

- Light and sound permit

- Open flame permit

- Parade permit

- Security and safety permit

- Sports permit

- Staging permit

- Temporary construction/shelter permit

No two communities have identical licensing, permits, practices, authorizing agencies, forms, filing schedules, or fees. You'll have to get familiar with the policies in areas you imagine you'll find work. While you can learn while you go along, you'll look much more professional if you have done your homework in advance, so you can tell your clients what to expect.

Event Insurance

The party planner, the vendors and the host may wish to carry some kind of insurance to protect themselves in the case that someone has too much to drink and drives home, or hurts themselves and decides to sue. There is insurance for the party itself that covers those involved.

There is also weather or cancellation insurance that reimburses the deposits and other expenses should the event have to be cancelled for some reason. Talk to your favorite insurance provider about the event-related and social host coverage they provide.

2.3   Creative Elements

Once you have hammered out the details of time, place and location, it's time for getting truly creative. You and your client will work together to develop interesting themes and beautiful or funky décor that will leave the guests in awe of the host — and you. In this section we'll cover:

- Party Theme

- Invitations

- Food and Drink

- Music and Entertainment

- Decorating

- Party Games/Activities

- Gift Bags

2.3.1   Choosing a Party Theme

A party theme is a unifying concept that flows through the party. It links the food and drink, the invitations, the décor and all the creative parts of the party together. A theme should have a cohesiveness that reflects the personality of the host, as well as the objective of the party.

Coming Up with Something Creative

You might think that by the time clients call a planner they already know what kind of theme they want for their party. Sometimes, but not always is this the case. Clients may want you to come up with all the ideas for them, and they'd better be original.

Nobody wants to be the "been there, done that" party planner in town. In addition to being able to form strong relationships with vendors, your ability to dream up and implement unique themes is probably the most important skill you can have.

Sometimes the theme will be basic: it's a sweet sixteen, it's a retirement party. Fair enough, but it's up to you to find ways to build from the basics. "Event themes are sometimes obvious, but often I try to put a new twist on them," says planner Kathleen Kellner. "I try to work with my client for inspiration and ideas. It can be as simple as a décor item that we build around, or even a certain color, to an idea around the guest of honor's personality," she continues.

Kellner told us about one memorable event she planned for a 40th birthday party. "I took different aspects of the guest of honor's personality –his love of sports, gambling and food – and created theme rooms in various areas of the host's spacious home. Guests were treated to a retrospective of the guest of honor's life thus far, with photos, food and beverage and entertainment appropriate for each of the rooms. It was like having several small parties that guests could circulate through and experience, as the rooms were all distinct."

Bernard Puccio remembers being desperate for an original theme for a May Day party. When he and Kennedy discovered that the roots of May Day were in Greek mythology, they decorated with caryatid statues and garlands of flowers hung from the chandeliers.

Contrast that with a party they planned at the Beverly Wilshire Regent Hotel in Beverly Hills. "We created a dance theme," Puccio recalls, "interspersing production dance styles between food courses — from the '20s Charleston, through the Latin periods, '40s swing, and '70s disco."

Types of Themes

A theme can be a popular TV show, book or movie, a specific food, a country or culture, a particular color, or certain pop culture icons. "I have created an entire event around a song or a décor idea, and my clients are always very pleased with the results," says Kathleen Kellner.

Here are some themes that are classics, or that are popular right now. You can use the theme "as is," or try to come up with ways to put a new spin on them to make them truly unique. The websites listed in section 3.2.1 also have articles and message boards dedicated to sharing the latest and greatest in party themes:

- Casino or poker night

- Cinderella/princess party

- Decade party (the '50s, the '80s)

- Girls only

- Hawaiian party

- Holiday or seasonal event

- Karaoke party

- Mardi Gras party

- Movie star party

- Oscar party

- Pajama party

- Sleepover party

- Spa/pampering party

- Sporting event party

- Toga party

- Wine tasting party

- "I don't need a reason to party" party

Of course, you can combine more than one theme, or put a unique twist on an old theme. Be warned that there is such a thing as overdoing it, though. "Don't 'over-theme' or be too obvious or cliché," cautions Kathleen Kellner. "Rather than trying to fit all of the theme ideas into an event, take a couple of elements and work with them."

> TIP: Even if your party's theme is not seasonal, it is wise to take the season into account when planning a theme. Certain foods and flowers will be in season (therefore fresher and cheaper), and the season will also have an effect on guests' attire and mood.

Pulling it all Together

When you have decided on a theme, then you need to think about how you will have all the elements of the party reflect that concept. You can go through the party elements listed in this section and brainstorm with your client ways that you could incorporate the theme.

Think about how the guests will experience each element with all five of their senses. Don't just consider how food will taste, but also how it will smell and look. How will those elements combine with the smells and décor of the rest of the party? You don't want the smell of fresh roses overwhelmed by your scented candles, for example.

Here's how Kathleen Kellner pulled together a "New York Club Scene" themed event for one of her clients. As you read her ideas, think about how you would have created this theme yourself:

> The event was held in a private residence with 150 guests. The invita-tions were simple and classic, the wording reflecting the casualness of

the event. Food was beautifully catered, but the menu included mini pizzas, mini hamburgers, quesadillas and other pub menu items.

The décor was yards and yards of black fabric on all walls of the rooms, with fluorescent tape accents between each fabric panel. I hired a local graffiti artist to create several large pieces of graffiti art on un-mounted canvas that was then stapled to the walls.

The rooms were lit with black light, and the overall effect was very striking and effective. The entertainment was a local rock band that does great covers of all the most popular club music, as well as a DJ who played in between band sets. Guests were in full party mode un-til five a.m.!

2.3.2   Creating and Sending Invitations

Invitations are the first hint that a party is going to have pizzazz. If you are working with a particular theme, invitations are a great way to in-troduce it. Many party planners offer invitation design or purchase as part of their services, and will also send the invites and collect RSVPs for their clients. Here's what you need to know.

Creating a Guest List

The first thing you need for invitations is a guest list supplied by your client. This list should include names and contact information for each guest. Even if the client has a list ready to hand to you, you should sit down with them and confirm the guests one by one.

As you review the list, keep an eye out for incomplete addresses or other possible typos. You should also confirm with your host that the addresses are as up to date as possible.

If budget or exclusivity is a concern, you may also help your client de-termine who should and should not be invited. Will you include spous-es on the invitation? Does "spouse" extend to longtime boyfriend? And really, what is meant by "longtime"?

Determining the types of guests to attend the party may be a matter of security or status. Parties for corporate management generally don't include the guys in the mailroom, and parties with celebrities in atten-dance don't include the children's gawking friends from school.

TIP: Sometimes VIP guests will be invited to arrive earlier for dinner or a reception, and the bulk of attendees (or another group altogether) will be asked to arrive a bit later for the dancing and socializing.

If you're planning a children's party, be sure to find out whether adults will be dropping off their children, acting as chaperones only, or staying as cake-eating guests. What may look like a guest list of 15 can quickly grow to 30 with a few well-meaning parents lagging behind to "help."

Total up how many invitations you will need to send, and confirm that number with the client. You should also get an idea of how much they want to spend per invite, so there are no surprises on the invoice. Encourage your client to plan on about one non-attendee per five invites, and invite more people than they hope will attend.

If you are planning a major event well in advance, you could send out a "save the date" postcard even earlier that alerts prospective guests to the fact that an invitation is on the way. These cards should hint at the theme or match the invitations in some way. It's also fun to make them intriguing, so the guests are eager to save the date for this event.

If you plan to print labels, the guest list needs to be typed and formatted so that can happen. Clerical temps or a secretarial service can create the computerized version of a list that will fit neatly on a mailing label. Expect to pay $25 or so per hour for data-entry services, unless you know a student who does odd jobs.

You can print the labels yourself on a home computer, or have a printer generate and/or affix them for you. Avery labels are a popular choice for mailing, and Microsoft Word comes with templates that conform to a code for each type of Avery label. If you want the print shop to do this for you, you'll need to burn a disc with the label information, and deliver that to them.

For last-minute parties, email or phone invitations might be a necessity. Check with your guest as to what they prefer, and make sure that you have a system in place to receive RSVPs as well. A web service called Evite (**www.evite.com**) allows you to create a database for your event and send invitations by email.

Invitation Content and Design

An invitation has specific content requirements: time, date, and place of the party, its purpose, and attire. The party guests should not have to guess at anything. The host should be identified, and the gift issue should be addressed, such as no gifts, or no flowers.

It should indicate what if any meal will be served. It needs to be very clear on how to RSVP. Arrangements and/or contact information for lodging, perhaps at a discount, could be part of the invitation. You may also want to include a map with driving and parking directions.

Creating an invitation could be as uncomplicated as picking a design from a local stationery store's catalog, however, custom-designed invitations are more usual when a professional planner and a theme are involved. You will work with a graphic designer or print shop to develop a concept and approve a design that reflects your chosen theme. Your client should be involved in the approval process, including the labels and stationery.

Consider each of the following, and how they affect the overall message:

- Paper stock
- Language
- Artwork
- Typeface
- Layout
- Size
- Color
- Envelope
- Stamp
- Seal
- Method of delivery

If the party is going to be elegant, then the invitation should be simple and classy as well. If the party is going to be tongue-in-cheek hilarious, then use your funny bone and some cute cartoons when your write it up. The invitation is a sign of things to come.

> **TIP:** Be aware that increased weight and size of an invitation means increased cost to your client in terms of postage.

If you are crafty and have the right materials, you can make invitations yourself. There are many books available on creating beautiful invitations, and you can also take classes at a stationery shop, craft store, or community college. If you go this route, remember that the invitations will have to look as professional as possible.

If you don't think handmade invitations are your thing, network to find someone (or a few people) you can source this task out to. If you have poor handwriting, you may also want to hook up with a calligrapher or just someone with nice writing, in case your client wants invites handwritten.

Depending on the client's taste and budget, invitations out of the box or from a catalog may be just right. You can accumulate a number of catalogs for your clients to browse through for ideas and inspiration, or if the event is far enough in advance, you can special-order them. You can also request single samples of invitations from manufacturers or vendors to show your clients.

Handling RSVPs

A way to respond to the invitation should be included or indicated in the invitation, such as an RSVP telephone number, email address or website, or self-addressed envelope with a response card. If you will offer guests a choice of entrées you need to include that in the response request as well.

As guest responses come in, somebody has to be responsible for putting names on the list of attendees, which means checking and processing snail mail, email, and telephone messages. For answering- machine RSVPs, there must be an appropriate message that facilitates clear guest responses. This is a service that many party planners choose to provide.

Be prepared for some guests who RSVP by phone to leave an additional message for the client/host, or have questions and comments that have nothing to do with responding to the invitation, or who make special requests.

"I have even had RSVPs that included letters from guests requesting whom they would or would not like to be seated with," says Bernardo Puccio. Don't ignore these messages — if they are not related to what you are handling, or if you don't feel comfortable deciding how to respond, pass them along to the host.

Inviting High-Profile Guests

You don't have to be in Hollywood or at some jet-set resort to have celebrities on hand at a party. Every town has its own version of high-profile people. It could be the mayor, the news anchor from the local TV station, a local beauty pageant winner, the community theater director, and so on.

"High profile guests usually attend with their own entourage," says Orin Kennedy. "And in a public space like a hotel we coordinate with their security or hire our own." You'll need to account for these extra bodies when you choose a space.

What's important operationally for you is to have security issues under control. A plan for handling traffic so that clusters of people don't crowd around somebody is one aspect of this. More generally, you want to keep gatecrashers from ruining everybody's good time.

Celebrity presence at a party can be a significant attendance draw. At some parties, such as charitable events, for example, party organizers will want their celebrity guests to be visible, because this can help generate publicity and interest in the goals of the organization. If that is the case, then you will also want to plan for a media presence, and a place for photo-taking.

Selling Tickets

Typically, tickets to parties are linked to charity and other nonprofit organization events and fundraising. A political or charitable party may be a $500-a-plate affair, or attendees may be invited to "buy a table."

Tickets might be substituted for invitations at some parties or used in addition to invitations at others.

You and the clients should be on the same page about the logistics of issues such as whether tickets (which may have to be designed and printed) are to be mailed to guests or there is to be a will-call table at the site. Who will staff such a table should also be determined.

Some organizations publish a finite number of tickets and then offer them for sale, anticipating the limitation on the size of the crowd. Other organizations do not necessarily limit the number of ticket sales. That's important to you because if the number of tickets sold exceeds the capacity of a room you have reserved, you may have to upgrade. It is important to plan for such a possibility when you book the venue reservation and to prepare the client for the possibility that the amount to be spent on venue reservation may change.

2.3.3   Food and Drink

It is a rare gathering that is not built around food and drink. A smart planner is very involved in the food and drink selections and service, no matter who caters the food, because unsatisfactory party foodservice is more likely to be blamed on a planner than on the people who cooked and served it.

Foodservice Options

Serving drinks of some kind is a must, and some food is also a given. Your client will decide whether they want to serve a sit-down multi-course dinner, a buffet-style spread, or simply stick with snacks and drinks. The time of the party will partially dictate the type and amount of food and drink required. If your host is on a budget, let him or her know that a breakfast or brunch can save money on food and drink, and is a unique time to throw a get-together too.

Get an approximate per-person budget from your client, and ask them if they have worked with a particular caterer in the past that they have liked. If not, you want to go to your list of vendors and see who is appropriate for that gathering. Look for someone who specializes in what your client has in mind, if possible.

Alternately, your client may prefer to make food on their own, or make some of the meal and order the rest. Suggest that they make whatever they have in mind in advance and freeze it, though, since there are many other things to tend to the day of the party.

Like all the other party elements listed in this section, your food selections should match your theme. There are many, many cookbooks devoted to the idea of entertaining, and they suggest entire meals that you can match to a theme. If there is no theme, match the food to the host's or guests' preferences, or style of party.

It's also trendy to present the food in a way that is surprising or fun. Cutting up food normally served whole into tiny bites with toothpicks, or serving french fries in paper cones is both attractive and unique. If you choose to serve hot appetizers, have some cold ones placed as well for guests who arrive late or want to keep on snacking.

Kathleen Kellner says that she loves to try to find non-traditional uses for items when she sets a table. "At one event the caterer served a trio of hors d'oeuvres on small ceramic wall tiles," she remembers.

The key to a successful food selection is variety and simplicity. Even things that seem a sure bet, such as a cheese platter, are not fool-proof. Work in as much variety to the menu as possible by serving smaller amounts of a greater selection of items.

Anything that can be presented "on the side," such as dressings and sauces, should be served that way. It's kind of like buying a coffee for someone you don't know very well. You get cream and sugar on the side and the biggest size available just in case, rather than trying to guess at what they want!

Using a Caterer

If you are using a venue such as a hotel that has a caterer they use, you may be limited to what they can create. If you have a few caterers in mind, arrange to meet with them to discuss a menu, and ask them to prepare a quote for your client. You may even choose to work with a few different caterers on one event if the menu is extensive.

You may not have a camera crew following you around the way Giada De Laurentiis does on the Food Network's program *Behind the Bash*, but it is quite routine to sample caterers' food before hiring them for a professionally planned party. If you don't like the food, there's no point in doing business with them, even if they are friendly and have the best price. Bernardo Puccio told us he might have as many as three tastings before being satisfied with food preparation. He says he especially dislikes heavy sauces, and the kind of cuisine where entrees are plopped onto beds of potatoes.

Caterers routinely create menus of meals that are priced on a per-person basis — for example, linguine primavera at $20, prime rib and fixings at $45, or a buffet spread at $35 per person. A planner is perfectly entitled to create a menu, however, that the venue or other caterers prepare according to specifications. Service providers understand the benefits and appeal of novelty and should be willing to meet a planner's specifications.

> **TIP:** If you can't find an independent caterer that suits your client, ask them for a list of their favorite restaurants, and contact them to see what catering they may or may not do.

Food may be placed on a table or served by wait staff. The second option is of course more expensive, but is a better option for food that is served hot. Check and double-check with what the caterer provides, and what your client has to rent or arrange for themselves. You should have a serving schedule arranged with the caterer, so they know what hour your host wants food to be served, or in what order. It's thoughtful to have additional food available towards the end of the party as well, especially if the event has run several hours. Think deserts or sweet appetizers, and break out the coffee and tea to give the hint that things are winding down.

Catering requires an up-front deposit of 50%. A cancellation that occurs a week before the scheduled date usually will not carry a penalty. Because of the perishable nature of food and the prep time cooking requires, you can expect to be penalized if you wait until shortly before the scheduled event to cancel a caterer.

Dietary Restrictions

Some party invitations ask guests to indicate food restrictions as well as menu choice. Food allergies can be harmful or fatal. Shellfish and nuts are especially risky, but allergies to dairy products, eggs, corn, wheat, and soy are also common. Cultural and religious customs may also affect menu selection, as well as vegetarian or vegan lifestyles.

"I'm always prepared to serve the vegetarian, and on occasion have to cater to ethnic or religious menu restrictions," says Bernardo Puccio. The best way of handling such issues is to help the client anticipate them early in the process.

Wait and/or buffet staff should be able to tell guests whether a dish contains a particular ingredient. When you're coordinating with a caterer, be clear about whether X ingredient is part of the package. Also be clear that you need to approve ingredient changes in any dish. Dishes that are on a self-serve buffet should be labeled – chicken with peanut sauce or mincemeat pie with brandy-mint sauce, for example – both to inform guests in general, and to warn allergic or abstinent people off a particular food selection.

Serving Alcohol

Whether alcohol is served at a party, and how it is served will be up to your client and their budget. If the client wants to serve alcohol, there are a number of ways this can be accomplished.

You can hire a bartender who will mix and serve drinks for the guests, who come up to the bar and order. Your client may wish this to be an open bar where all drinks are complimentary, or a cash bar when guests must pay per drink.

For their adult parties, Puccio Designs usually recommends an open bar for cocktails, and wine with dinner. The wealthier the client and attendee list, the more likely your parties are to follow that model. As a matter of etiquette, an open bar at a party is generally expected these days, unless there are hundreds of people attending.

Sometimes it's possible to arrange a reduced fee cash bar, when the client agrees to pay a portion of each drink so that the guest can purchase it at a reduced amount. For example, if a mixed drink regularly costs $6, the host can agree to co-pay $3 per drink so that guests can purchase their drinks for a more reasonable $3.

Another alternative is a limited open bar, where all drinks are free but the selection is limited. Your client might choose to serve only wine or beer, and maybe rye, vodka and tequila. This gives guests a reasonable selection of drinks to choose from, but will usually keep costs down. You can use a variety of mixers to make it seem like there is more selection.

If your host doesn't want to have to have a bartender on hand, it's also acceptable to put bar ingredients out on the bar, and allow guests to select, mix and pour their own drinks. This is an especially good option if pre-mixed drinks are being served (e.g. pitchers of sangria for a Mexican party), and simplifies the process.

Yet another option is to have wandering wait staff who take orders and return with drinks. Your client will pay extra for this service, but it's a nice touch, and saves the host worrying about whether everyone's glass is full.

On average, expect guests to consume about two drinks an hour for the first half of an evening party, and one drink an hour after that. Any fluctuations from this norm should balance each other out. Of course, if your host indicates to expect any different, go with their knowledge of their guests. And at any rate, it's better to have more than you need than to run out.

The Evite website mentioned in section 2.3.2 has an online calculator you can use to estimate the amount of alcohol to purchase for a party based on a number of different factors. Find it at **www.evite.com** (click on "Entertaining" and look for the "Planning Tools" section).

Your party has to comply with prevailing liquor laws. Local and state licensing and permit regulations may be an issue if your venue is public and not licensed to dispense liquor. In some communities a temporary or "picnic" liquor license for $50 to $200 will be all you need. But other regulations may also apply — for example, local laws may require you to hire bartenders to dispense drinks. If there is a public or quasi-public aspect to your event and if underage guests are present, you can also expect that inspectors with legal enforcement may show up from time to time.

To accommodate non-drinkers and promote responsible consumption, have a selection of equally attractive non-alcoholic drinks available, as well as water. The key is to make your non-alcoholic selections as enticing as the alcoholic ones. Check out the "non-alcoholic" section of a drink mixing guide, and get creative.

Bar Supplies

If your client is supplying and stocking the bar for their party, here are some of the supplies they may want to consider having on hand. You can go over this list with them and see what they need to put on their party:

- After-dinner drinks

- Assorted glassware

- Beer

- Blender
- Can/bottle openers
- Citrus twists and wedges
- Corkscrew
- Drink mixing guide (e.g. Mr. Boston Official Bartender's & Party Guide)
- Drink tickets
- Ice
- Ice buckets/caddies
- Ice tongs
- Long stirring spoon
- Mixers
- Napkins and coasters
- Onions, olives, cherries, celery
- Pitchers
- Shakers
- Shot glasses
- Spirits
- Straws, stirrers, spears, and toothpicks
- Wine
- Worcestershire, horseradish, salt

2.3.4   Music and Entertainment

Entertainment options are as varied as party themes, but planners will agree that music is a must at most parties. The kind of music you arrange will depend on the demographics of the party guests. You and the host might consider any or a mix of the following:

- A live band

- An orchestral trio

- A DJ spinning tunes

- A soloist

- A pre-recorded mix CD

- A selection of favorite albums

Music is another area where you can let your creative juices flow. The type of music should fit the theme or expected atmosphere of the party. A band, DJ, or sound system can all have a different impact on the atmosphere of the event.

You may want to suggest different types of music and different sound levels for different parts of the party. While low background music is nice for the cocktail hour, you will want to pump up the volume if the guests want to dance.

Someone (quite possibly you) should be in charge of keeping it at the right level and on the right programming track. Do a quick sound check before the party starts to make sure everything is plugged in right and ready to go. If there is a remote control for the volume, keep it on you just in case.

Musical styles may be a consideration. Bernardo Puccio believes that strings and harp music are a romantic and elegant touch, and that DJ programming tends to be more suited to limited budgets, teen parties, or a period-themed party. "For cocktails I prefer piano or a trio," he says, "or nothing, if the sound level of talking is expected to be loud."

The quality of music and the content of the programming take on the most significance at parties where there is dancing. "The right band for dancing is dependent on the age group of your guests," says Orin Kennedy. "I also ask for band's song list and pick the music myself."

Live Music

If you are going to recommend live musicians to your clients, you need to know in advance that they are talented, and the right fit for the event.

You can hold a couple of audition sessions to meet with the musicians and assess their skills, or you can ask other vendors for referrals.

Another option is to try to get out and see some local bands from time to time. It is not unusual for musicians who get gigs at clubs and restaurants to come prepared with business cards, CDs, and press kits. If you enjoy a performance, you will want to make contact with the performers in between sets or after the show.

You can put together a contact sheet for each act that includes their contact info, rates, availability, and if they supply all their own equipment, and attach it to their press kit. Keep these on file for the future, and update them periodically.

Entertainment

Many different entertainment options are available for parties. Clowns, magicians, and novelty athletes often specialize in kids' parties, although some gear their act towards adults. Entertainment can add real pizzazz to a party, especially if it fits in with the overall theme. Some fun options include:

- Animal trainers
- Caricaturists
- Casino dealers
- Comedians
- Dancers
- Fortune tellers
- Hypnotists
- Impressionists or look-alikes
- Movie or TV show screenings
- Masseuses
- Lounge-style piano player
- Psychics
- Spa service technicians

You develop resources like these in fairly straightforward ways. Puccio Designs uses local party directories, the Internet, and recommendations. Deals are made because Kennedy or Puccio has seen the performers' work, "whether in person, in photos, or by attending an event," according to Kennedy.

An Emcee

Parties that are complex enough to be planned commonly have a structured program of some kind. Even a simple retirement party has a structure, since one or more guests may toast the retiree with a speech before the entire crowd of guests, and awards may be presented.

An emcee "positions" parties for attendees, reminding them of the event's purpose and guiding them through the various phases and aspects of the event. He or she may be the voice behind the crowd's movement from cocktails to dining, from dining to after-dinner speech, and from there to dancing. The emcee will be the one to thank any volunteers, and may remind the guests to sign the guestbook for the party.

Kennedy says an emcee is a must for a planned party that has a corporate or charitable purpose, and the planner may be the one to recruit that person. "Sometimes I've even taken on that responsibility," he adds. Ask the host if they have someone in mind who might make a good emcee, or have a few people of your own for backups. A local radio host, for example, might be willing to emcee the occasional event.

2.3.5   Decorating

Decorating for the party can be simple, or transport guests to another world, depending on the look you are going for. Decorating for your own child's party might be limited to a printed paper tablecloth and colored streamers, but as a professional party planner it's up to you to take things up a notch.

Consider how color, mood and theme factor into the selection of décor elements such as:

- Centerpieces
- Lighting

- Linens

- Flowers

- Serving trays

- Wall and floor coverings

- Furniture

- Place cards and menus

- Knick-knacks or conversation pieces

"Ambience," says Orin Kennedy, "is so important. It is achieved through careful color coordination of table settings, flowers, and background décor." Especially important, Kennedy notes, is the lighting, which can create extraordinary effects.

You need to have some initial concepts and décor to match. Pick the vendor's brains too, especially when you are just starting out in your career. Make sure all your decorative and creative influences complement each other.

Kathleen Kellner tells us about her creative décor for an anniversary event: "The traditional gift for a first anniversary is paper, so I had a local Origami artist create some beautiful pieces of Origami that I used for the cocktail table centerpieces. The hostess loved the idea, and the pieces fit in well with the simple yet elegant décor I had created for the room."

Flowers are always a popular decorative touch, since they add both beauty and scent. You may decide to hire a florist to handle flower selection and delivery, but it is advised that you have some ideas of what your client is looking for before setting a meeting. Know whether they want their flowers to be understated, or to make a statement.

"I am all for simple elegance and the 'less is more' approach to décor. I always try to work with fresh floral, and high quality décor items. I would rather purchase unique pieces than rent tired centerpieces from décor rental companies," says Kathleen Kellner.

Different lighting from what we are used to every day creates mood and ambiance. Because they serve the double-role of decoration and

alternative light source, candles are a popular choice for party lighting. From tea lights to scented candles to pillars, candles can transform any space. Tiki torches, paper lanterns and colored bulbs are fun choices as well for themed events.

Lighting specialists can create light or light-and-sound shows of various kinds. They should be asked to develop a presentation that fits with the theme of the party. Puccio Designs has incorporated moving lights such as mirrored balls, chase lights (small lights that flash in sequence), follow spots, and wall projections of photos and logos into its decoration schemes.

Lighting-related décor also has to be consistent with the electrical capacity of the venue — probably no problem at a hotel ballroom, but potentially a problem on a great big lawn. There are retailers who specialize in this arena. Have a list of questions ready before you buy or rent decorative party lights. Specialty contractors of all kinds may have to bring their own power source.

When you design décor, keep the guests' mobility and safety in mind. The party room should not be an obstacle course, but should be easy for guests to navigate in terms of space, layout, safety, and common sense. You don't want a lot of crepe-paper flowers floating around in a room where the banquet tables have open-flame candles as part of the centerpieces. Indeed, if there will be any open flame in the room, you need to be able to meet the fire marshal's standards. Fire extinguishers should be handy, and candle holders need to be steady.

The size of the party room comes into play as well, not only for reasons of décor but also for safety reasons cited above. Nor should elements of the decoration impinge on the space that guests have to mingle.

TIP: To create the perfect party ambiance, you may need to move furniture around, move it right out of the room, or rent something different — e.g., bean bag chairs for a 70s party. Ideally, though, you want to mostly work with what the host or venue already has.

Photographers and Videographers

Parties that are fancy enough to be planned are parties that attendees want to remember. "Photographers are a must," declares Bernardo Puccio. "People want to record their experience for their personal history, in both still photography and video."

That does not necessarily mean you want a lot of pushy paparazzi running around. It does mean you use one or more photographers who shoot candid shots of people at a party or a group shot of all of the guests. Some guests may even want to purchase prints of selected shots. Video records of big parties are also very common. You might want to shoot a specific portion of the event, or just people having a good time.

2.3.6   Party Games/Activities

In general, games and activities are more likely to be featured with children's parties than adult parties. But that's not to say that games are not appropriate at certain types of adult parties, such as baby showers, bachelor and bachelorette parties, or parties with a games theme.

For children's parties, the games should be age-appropriate, and should not be overly competitive. With young children, everyone should win a small prize. Some popular selections include the following, which you can customize or adapt to fit a theme. If you are unfamiliar with any of these games, do a quick search on the Internet for rules and adaptations:

- Craft-making activities

- Duck, duck, goose

- Hot potato

- Musical chairs

- Pin the tail on the donkey

- Piñata

- Scavenger hunt

- Tag or hide-and-seek

- Telephone (also known as "gossip")

- Water balloon toss

For adult parties, look for games that don't require everyone to be huddled around a game board, or you'll end up with a lack of attention and/or guests with sore backs.

If games are what your clients want you should accommodate them, but warn them that sometimes they don't go as planned. People are people — they get pouty when they lose, or may be overly critical or overly competitive. Or a game might simply be a bust. Tell your host to be flexible on how long games are played, or if they take place at all.

Trivia games are often popular, as are games based on game shows and drawing games. Cranium, Scene It, Would You Rather, and games with DVD content are all popular selections right now. The following websites have a great variety of fun party games you can suggest to your client, if party games are on the agenda. Be aware that many adult games can be a bit risqué, so they need to match the type of guests.

- *Party Game Central*
  www.partygamecentral.com

Party Game Ideas
www.partygameideas.com

- *Party Games Etc.*
www.party-games-etc.com

In place of games, planned activities can also be popular. These can be anything from spa treatments and blackjack tables, to pony rides or bouncer castles. If there are activities that are a fit with your theme and the budget is there, planned activities can turn a ho-hum get-together into the talk of the town.

And The Prize Goes to...

Where there are games, there are prizes. Even if it's only something small or jokey, prizes make playing competitive games more fun. You can look for unique, inexpensive prizes at a dollar store, game store, book store, gadget store or organization store. The prizes, like all other elements of the party, should reflect the theme.

At parties for children, it's often a good idea to give prizes to the winners at the same time that gift bags are handed out to the other children. That way everyone feels like a winner.

2.3.7   Gift Bags for Guests

Whether gift bags are given out depends on client preferences, budget, and the kind of party. Especially with a theme party they are a nice touch, and for children's parties they are generally expected. The items in your gift bag don't have to be expensive, but they should be trendy, useful, or cute, and appropriate to the reason for the party.

Everything from souvenir glassware to personalized stationery to best-selling books to key chains are possibilities. For a children's birthday party the choice may be some kind of toy or candy. Like prizes, gift bag items can be sourced cheaply at dollar or gadget stores. You can also visit party supply stores to see what they have to offer.

If your client doesn't want to do gift bags but still wants to get something for the guests, suggest a door prize or raffle draw for something more expensive, such as sporting event tickets or a day at the spa. Gift baskets can be an elaborate version of a party favor that you can transform into an added-value signature and revenue source if you make them yourself.

> **TIP:** For lavish, big-budget affairs, the invitation can include a gift as well, as an enticement to attend. The invitation gift should reflect the theme of the party or the planned décor somehow.

Puccio Designs, Inc., is always on the lookout for unique table decorations that double as gifts. Among the most popular Puccio and Kennedy have used are miniature frames with the guests' names and pictures used as place cards. What a great idea for parties such as reunions, where guests haven't seen each other in a while!

Match your gift bags to your guest list — you may need different bags for males and females, depending on what you put in them. You don't have to stick to a traditional bag for the gifts, either. Chinese take-out boxes or a drawstring pouch are some creative touches to consider.

Keep in mind that in the U.S. gift bags containing expensive gifts can be taxable in certain contexts, and are considered as income equal to the market value of the bag and its contents. To find out more about the tax implications of gift bags as income visit the IRS website at **www.irs. gov/newsroom/article/0,,id=161153,00.html**.

2.4 Getting Organized

Of course planning parties is hectic — that's why party planners exist! You will have a secret weapon, though: superior organizational skills and techniques to keep everything running smoothly.

2.4.1 How to Establish a Timeline

A timeline is a detailed list of what tasks need to get done before a party, and when they need to be done by. The way to create a party timeline is to do what's called backward mapping. Backward mapping begins with the party date, a calendar, and clarity about what has to be done. Work backward from the date of the event, building in sufficient time to accomplish specific tasks. Some events are less complicated than others, so they will require less lead time. For example, if your party date is August 11, written invitations need to go out a minimum of two to three weeks before that, to give people enough time to make personal plans and RSVP to the event.

> **TIP:** As a general rule, corporate or sponsored parties require more lead time (about twice as much) than parties for individuals. The more you have to deal with a committee-based approval process, the more time you will need.

The relationships that you have built with vendors will partly determine how efficiently they can fulfill your various orders. This guide will look at relationship-building with vendors later in section 5.3.

Use the *Sample Party Planning Timeline* on the next two pages as a guide. Keep in mind that not every party will involve everything listed —and that some parties will involve more to-do items as needed. For corporate events you may need to build in more time for the approval process.

2.4.2   Your To-Do Lists

Party planners usually have pages and pages of to-do lists for each event they organize. Your at-home to-do lists are usually pretty simple, and look a bit like this:

- Fold laundry

- Book doctor's appointment

- Clean out closet

- Buy gift for Mom

These lists are simple reminders of things that need to be done by you sometime soon. When you are organizing something with as many details as a party, though, your to-do lists need more information, so you know what order to do them in, who else may be doing tasks, and when they need to be done by.

Sample Party Planning Timeline

5 to 8 Weeks in Advance

- ❑ Establish date and time
- ❑ Establish general guest profile, number of guests
- ❑ Reserve group discounts for travel, lodging
- ❑ Establish party structure/type and theme
- ❑ Discuss possible venues and place reservations
- ❑ Establish budget
- ❑ Get invitation list contact information
- ❑ Begin design of invitation

4 to 6 Weeks in Advance

- ❑ Reserve caterer
- ❑ Menu approval
- ❑ Decoration/design approval
- ❑ Table décor
- ❑ Invitation or program design approved
- ❑ Begin draft of party agenda

3 to 4 Weeks in Advance

- ❑ Food and drink menu finalized
- ❑ Invitations printed and mailed
- ❑ Finalize décor and seating arrangements

❏ Identify security requirements, contract with venue, third-party security services

❏ Schedule wait/service staff

❏ Schedule/contract videographers, photographers, related event services

❏ Contract for floral designs; schedule floral installations

❏ Printing of menus, cards, labels, etc.

❏ Structure guest support services as needed (childcare, cloakroom)

❏ Schedule installation of décor, sound and staging

❏ Arrange for clean-up if needed

❏ Schedule entertainment (DJ, emcee, other performers)

1 to 2 Weeks Before the Party

❏ Create nametags and place cards

❏ Seating arrangement

❏ Order cake if needed

❏ Arrange to rent any necessary items

2 Days Before the Party/Day of the Party

❏ Décor installations

❏ Rehearsal if necessary

❏ Food and beverage prep, delivery, service setup

❏ Meet and discuss event with staff

❏ Call host to ensure all is well

TIP: These kinds of to-do lists are also called "critical paths" in business jargon.

You may want to have separate to-do lists for different aspects of the party, such as décor, entertainment, etc. Lists are also useful to remember the supplies you need to buy (groceries or décor), people you need to contact, and so on.

You can create your own to-do lists in word-processing programs, or use some of the party planning software mentioned in section 5.1.2. You can use the *Sample To-Do List* on the next page as a starting point.

2.4.3 The Party Agenda

Whether your event is an hour-long bon voyage gathering or an all-day barbeque, it's important to know the order events are going to take place in, and an approximate time they should happen at. Your client may tell you, "I don't need an agenda, I just want people to show up and have a good time," but you'll need to nail down a few details just the same. It helps to point out that even an event as simple as a preschooler's birthday party has an agenda of sorts. For example:

12:45 p.m.	Children's music turned on; front door opened
1:00 p.m.	Guests begin to arrive
1:15 p.m.	Free play with toys
2:00 p.m.	Pin the tail on the donkey
2:15 p.m.	Musical chairs
2:30 p.m.	Cake is served; loot bags distributed
2:45 p.m.	Presents opened
3:15 p.m.	Guests begin to leave

For an adult party, your client is likely to have definitive views on what hour dinner will be served, when speeches will take place, and what time the coffee will go on signaling guests that things are winding down. "Never do a party," says Bernardo Puccio, "without a detailed script or program timed from the rehearsals until the closing moments."

Sample To-Do List

Party Element:				
Task	Person Responsible	Due Date	Notes	Completed

The more high-end the party, the more likely it will be that you will have a scripted program and a schedule to go with it. The content of the program may vary from awards presentations to after-dinner speaking to a panel discussion to a concert to a movie. Music, sound, light cues, and so forth must be planned for, and everyone concerned should be on the same page.

Orin Kennedy's longtime work in the TV business ensures that the programs at Puccio Design's parties run smoothly. "I am the producer, writer and director," he says, "from timing the food course to the entertainment to the lighting and sound cues." He writes all the cues directly on a party "program," which serves as the script.

2.4.4   Floor Plan and Layout

A floor plan determines installation of entertainment staging, seating arrangements, etc. If you have vendors arriving with flowers, other decorations, cakes, food or equipment, it's useful to have one complete floor plan that you can hand them (or fax them in advance) that shows where they are to set up. This saves you a lot of hand-holding on the day of the party.

When you are drafting a floor plan, this is also a good time to select a place for guest coats to be stored, and decide how your host wishes to accommodate smokers. Having a protocol for smokers, such as a designated area and butt disposal equipment, will prevent your host from picking up discarded butts days later, or worse, having someone light up uninvited in their home.

Slides, film, PowerPoint setup, and the like may also have to be accommodated. When the speaker says "Kill the lights," will somebody be prepared to do that, or will various people be looking for wall switches because you didn't mark them on your floor plan?

If the purpose is to have a party honoring a politician, for example, then you probably need to reserve an appropriately decorated space for handshakes and photography. If the objective is to have those who are photographed with the guest of honor donate money to a cause, then you need to plan for a table or room for money to be accepted and accommodate those who will staff that duty.

Pulling off the technical elements of a program can be tricky if pre-party access to the venue is restricted and setup time is limited. You must build time into your setup plans to check lights and light cues, sound system and cues, and staging. Audiovisual equipment – film, video, slide show, microphones, cameras – must be cued up. Such features as balloon releases have to be timed properly and their mechanical mechanisms primed properly.

Orin Kennedy has everyone report for a production meeting an hour before the start of the event, and he runs the rehearsal and the event program itself. At minimum he books the space a day before the run-through.

2.4.5   Typical Party Supplies

Myra Taylor, whose area of specialty is special-event planning, told us about one of her most memorable projects, a man-of-the-year dinner honoring former President Ronald Reagan. The black-tie reception was supposedly all set. It was an elegant party for a dozen or so movers and shakers, and the fact that a board member had gotten someone to donate fine wines for the occasion was a real coup.

Came the day, and the limos and black ties began to arrive. Suddenly it became clear that the party had one problem: Neither the caterer nor the bartender had a corkscrew. And there sat cases and cases of fine wine, unopened. A fast trip to a liquor store a block away solved the problem, but had the reception been located far from a retail outlet instead of in an urban neighborhood, that one detail could have turned into a disaster.

To prevent disasters of your own, refer to the *Party Supplies Checklist* on the next few pages for a list of supplies that are to be found at virtually any party. You may want to purchase some of them to have on hand, or simply review the list with your client a few days prior to the event.

2.5   At the Party

As liaison between client and all of the other vendors and support staff who are involved in transforming the original ideas for the party into reality, the party planner is the one who holds clients' hands as the curtain goes up on the action.

Party Supplies Checklist

❑ Alka Seltzer	❑ Aprons
❑ Ashtrays	❑ Aspirin
❑ Balloons	❑ Banquet tables
❑ BBQ grill(s)	❑ Beer keg + CO2 charger
❑ Blue ice packs	❑ Bottle openers
❑ Bottled water	❑ Cabaret tables
❑ Candles	❑ Card decks
❑ Card tables	❑ CD changer/player
❑ Centerpieces	❑ Chairs
❑ Cleaning supplies	❑ Coasters
❑ Cocktail caddy(ies)	❑ Cocktail napkins
❑ Coffee urn/tea setup	❑ Cooler(s)
❑ Corkscrew(s)	❑ Dinnerware
❑ Door prize	❑ Dry ice
❑ Fire extinguisher(s)	❑ Flashlight
❑ Flowers, vases, etc.	❑ Foodservice vessels
❑ Fruit juice	❑ Game supplies
❑ Glassware	❑ Guest towels (bathrooms)
❑ Guestbook & pen	❑ Hand carts
❑ Hand towels	❑ Heating lamps
❑ Hotpads	❑ Hotplates

❑ Ice	❑ Ice buckets
❑ Liquor	❑ Magic markers
❑ Matches	❑ Memo pads, cards
❑ More ice	❑ Music system
❑ Nametags	❑ Napkin rings
❑ Napkins	❑ Paper cups
❑ Paper towels	❑ Pens & pencils
❑ Place cards	❑ Place mats
❑ Punch bowl & cups	❑ Recycle signs
❑ Service dishes	❑ Snacks
❑ Soda, cocktail mixers	❑ Styrofoam cups
❑ Table décor	❑ Table linen, skirts
❑ Tables	❑ Thank-you notes
❑ Toilet paper	❑ Toothpicks
❑ Trash bags & bins	❑ Trays
❑ Utensils	❑ Utility towels/rags
❑ Voice amplification	❑ Warming plates
❑ Wine	❑ Yet more ice

"I am always on site before, during and after each event I produce. I am always very careful to give clear instruction to all staff working the event that if there are any questions or concerns, that they are to come to me and not the host of the event," explains Kathleen Kellner.

Everything should be in place by this time, and the client should have nothing to worry about except having a good time with friends, family, and colleagues.

2.5.1   Handling the Unexpected

All sorts of unexpected things can arise at a party, from uninvited guests, to inebriated guests, to fights or disagreements, to running out of a key supply. If you provide on-site service, the party planner's job is to quickly and professionally handle any unexpected events.

A good plan is to ask your host in advance how they would like to handle some of the more common occurrences, so you can leap into action without taking them away from enjoying their role as host. You should also arrive early to scope things out. Make sure that the walkway is shoveled, the dog is out of sight, and the outdoor lights are on, and that everything is just so.

> **TIP:**   You can also use this "alone time" to snap a few pictures of the set up, with your client's permission. Add these photos to your portfolio.

Difficult guests can be a challenge to handle. Orin Kennedy says he has had to deal with a number of contentious guests, "especially those who don't like their table placement, or don't want to be seated with a particular person." In fact, he adds, table seating can be the biggest single problem a party planner has to tackle once a party is under way, "especially amongst people who get together on a regular basis... believe it or not."

Guests who have had too much to drink present special challenges as well. Sometimes intoxicated guests can be brought down to earth, but if their condition combines with confrontation, then it may be necessary to bring security personnel or even police into the picture, as discreetly as possible.

Accidents are another possibility. Falls or other mishaps may require medical attention. If your party is being held at a hotel, calling 911 or finding a doctor or nurse in the house may be relatively easy. You should also ensure that your know where your host keeps medical supplies, or have some on hand yourself.

The need to plan for security of party guests may come up when celebrities are involved. Security was a special concern at the *Ally McBeal* 100th episode party, because it was held shortly after the 2001 World

Trade Center attacks, and was packed with star power. "We had the entire cast present," Puccio Designs' Kennedy recalls, "including the producer's wife [Michelle Pfeiffer] and high-profile entertainers such as Bon Jovi."

The keys to handling any unexpected event are to be prepared in advance (as much as is possible); to keep your cool; to handle things discreetly; and to deflect involvement from the host. Ideally, in many cases your client will not even be aware of a mishap until after the party is over.

In order to be ready to handle common emergencies, you should carry a list of emergency contacts, supplies and information with you, such as:

- 24-hour plumber phone number

- Cell phone

- Dial-a-Bottle phone number

- Driving services phone number

- Extra garbage bags

- Fire department phone number

- First aid kit

- List of stain removal techniques

- Lock service phone number

- Police phone number

- Spare clothing

- Taxi (several companies) phone number

- Toilet paper

- Tow truck phone number

- Vendors' phone numbers

You should also keep some stain removers and backup linens in your car, just in case there is a "red wine incident."

It's inevitable that, at some point in your party planning career, something will happen that you are unprepared for, or that you don't plan for or handle quite right. Rather than beat yourself up over it, treat every disaster as a learning opportunity, and a chance to make sure it never happens again.

2.5.2   Cleaning Up

If the venue, caterer, or host doesn't supply cleaning services, that task will fall to you. Clarify and budget for cleanup responsibilities in your agreements. Be sure that janitorial and other cleaning services are among the vendors that you check out when you assemble your roster of prospective subcontractors.

The best plan of attack is to arrange to clean up discreetly while the party is going on. Empty garbage and ashtrays as receptacles fill up rather than letting them overflow, and remove dirty dishes and glasses. This task doesn't have to fall to you as party planner — you can even hire some neighborhood teenagers to assist you if the budget is tight.

You'll make your job easier if there is already a place designated for empty bottles and cans. Otherwise they tend to pile up on counters and any available space. For outdoor parties, a lined garbage can labeled "recycling" will save a lot of cleaning up the next day.

Some bashes may even be so big and complicated that they call for a big truck to haul away the waste. You should be able to gauge whether that's true of a project fairly early on in the planning process. Check to see whether your city offers custom waste-removal service.

2.5.3   Following Up With the Host

The day after the party, give the host a call or email to make sure that they were satisfied with the way the party went. If your host has any concerns about the venue or the services, it's your job to follow up on the complaint. Alternately, you can pass along any words of praise to the vendors as well, to help you with your relationship-building.

You should also send a handwritten thank-you note to your client that is warmly written. Planner Sandra Dingler follows up with emails and thank-you notes after every event. She has been known to take a baby gift by to a repeat customer who had a new baby, long after the baby shower Dingler planned for her.

"I really do think personal notes are important," Dingler says, citing the advantages to customer retention. "You don't have to start over from scratch. We have people who have been our customers for 10 years, and their kids are calling us now."

Sample Thank-You Note

Dear Darla,

Thank you very much for the opportunity to work together with you to plan Jim's 40th birthday party. I'm sure you'll agree the look on his face was priceless. I was so happy to hear that you had a wonderful time, as well as receiving so many compliments on the event.

I would be happy to extend my services to you in the future for any entertaining you decide on. I have enclosed a few business cards for you to keep on file or pass along to friends.

Kind regards,
Paula Party Planner

3. Preparing for Your Career

Now that you know what the job entails, you're probably eager to get started with your new career. Although a lot of party planning abilities are those you may already have, it helps to take some time to assess where your strengths lie, and where you could use some improvement.

This chapter will introduce you to the skills you'll need as a party planner, and give you a variety of resources to help you develop them. We'll look at both formal and informal training options, and how to get some primary experience that will prepare you to run your own party planning business when you are ready.

3.1 Skills You Will Need

There are a few specific skills needed for the field of party planning. To be a big hit on the party scene, you will need to know party etiquette, have top-notch organizational and interpersonal skills, and keep yourself educated on the latest in entertainment trends. Outlined in this section is some necessary knowledge, as well as tips to help you perfect these skills.

3.1.1   Party Etiquette

They say etiquette never goes out of style, and that's definitely true when it comes to hosting a party. Etiquette might seem like a bunch of stuffy rules, but the fact is that party etiquette exists because it helps hosts and guests enjoy the event, right through from the planning to the plate-washing.

Your client will have hired you as a party expert, and so may turn to you on questions of etiquette. You will need to be ready to answer etiquette questions related to addressing invitations, setting tables, seating couples, making toasts, and getting that last guest to leave without making her feel like she was tossed to the curb. You may also be the one to step in and handle inebriated guests, or discreetly handle paying the bill at the end of the night.

While etiquette usually dictates how a situation should be handled, you will want to balance protocol with what your client feels is right. "Your job as a planner is to advise the client on what the 'etiquette rules' are, but always go with what the client desires," says Jill Hawkins of Miller-Hawkins Productions. "What the client wants is what is important."

This means that you have to check with your client before you handle any dicey situation. Find out in advance how they would like to handle unwanted guests, for example. Some experts will suggest that you should quietly set another plate and offer drinks, while others advocate that you ask whoever brought them to leave immediately. It's always better to know what your client wants than to guess.

Any handbook on entertaining will have a section on party etiquette that you can learn from. Alternately, any handbook on etiquette will have a dining or entertaining section to refer to. Also, the website Party411 has a resident "Etiquette Queen" to answer your etiquette-related questions, and her answers to previous questions are archived online. Visit **www.party411.com/queen.html**.

To get you started learning your own party etiquette, here are some helpful tips:

- When more than 10 guests will be attending, have assigned seats, or at least assigned tables. Having assigned seats eliminates confusion, awkwardness, and delays. Knowing where they are sitting is one less thing for the party guests to worry about.

- Guests should also have no less than 24 inches of space to themselves when seated at a table. The centerpiece should be low enough that guests can see each other.

- There is a protocol for addressing invitations, particularly when you are dealing with people of rank, such as doctors or the local mayor. Look up the correct form of address before you write them.

- Regardless of how small or short the gathering, every party should have food and drink available to guests. If dinner will not be served immediately, appetizers are a must.

- Cutlery is arranged at each place setting from outside (first used) to inside.

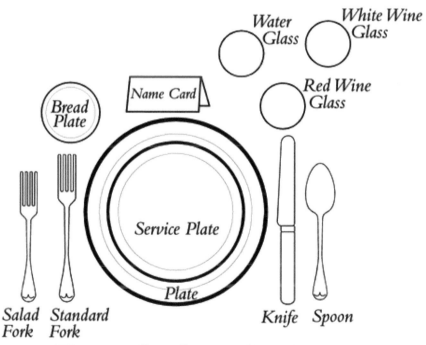

Formal Place-Setting

- Wait staff should always be tipped. Fifteen to twenty percent is the average. Make sure that a tip is not included in the bill to avoid double-tipping.

- Keep in mind when dealing with your clients that cultural differences can be an issue. Make sure you ask questions about cultural traditions that may affect party events or protocol.

- A thank-you card should be sent for each and every gift received. You can order the stationery for your client, but it would be impolite of you to write them — they should be handwritten by the host if possible.

- Finally, don't forget your own manners. Send a thank-you note to your client after the event. Include some business cards they can pass along to friends.

3.1.2 Organizational Skills

Party planning is a "details" business. Not just everyday details, either, but every, single, little, tiny detail. Only an organizational expert can make sure everything is handled right and on time. And organizing parties begins with organizing yourself.

One reason that people hire party planners is because there are so many things to coordinate when hosting a gathering. We have heard stories of parties at elegant mansions at which the caterer arrived to discover that the ovens in the kitchen weren't working (how would rich people who don't do their own cooking know that?).

As you grow more successful, you could even be planning a number of events at the same time. You could be booking venues for one party, at the same time as ordering supplies and organizing guest lists for another. Without a good system in place to ensure each detail is handled appropriately and on time, you could make mistakes — and there is little room for errors when it comes to keeping your clients happy.

Advice for Staying Organized

These days you have a choice about whether your own systems are paper or digital, but some mix of both is usually the best. Technology has a special way of failing us right when we need it the most, so having a paper copy of some items on hand is wise. On the other hand, taking advantage of digital organizers, spreadsheets, and planning software will save you time, and allow you to take on more clients.

Whatever system you use, it is crucial that you keep your files in order and updated. With either a computer or physical filing system, you should keep one main folder (or even a three-ring binder) for each party you organize, or at least one per client. Create subfolders or subsections for different aspects of the job, including the guest list and seating chart; the venue's information; supplies and decorations; menus and/or caterers; itineraries; and any other important facets to the job.

Dumping everything in one messy folder is a recipe for disaster — a lesson that most party planners have to learn the hard way. "I keep information files for all my suppliers as well as a business card binder which I usually carry with me when I am working," says planner Kathleen Kellner.

Use detailed checklists to make sure you have all the details of your event properly handled: invitations, guest lists, seating charts, the venue, menus and beverages, decorations, entertainment, and party favors or gifts. You read about how to draft effective to-do checklists in section 2.4.2 of this guide.

Your computer offers you other ways to stay organized, including a filing system for your email account. Set up folders within your inbox so that you can find correspondence relating to each event. "In an email account, each event should have its own folder, with subfolders for topics that have a lot of communication," says Paula Lundgren of Brainstorm Creative Business Services. "Rules can be set up to put emails from people specific to each event right into that event's email folder."

If you function well in today's high-tech world, you may want to buy a personal digital assistant (PDA). Their standard uses include scheduling (you can plan several years in advance), and an address/telephone book. More advanced features include text messaging, email and Internet access, and even spreadsheets and databases.

If you are more of a low-tech person, a day planner or calendar is still a good way to keep yourself organized. There are many brands of these to choose from as well, so make sure you pick one that allows you to not only record booked events, but include specific information, such as the occasion, time, location, phone number, names, and directions.

Traci Romano, of The Romano Group Event Planning + Design, says it helps to follow the "only touch it once" rule when it comes to the many papers that will flow into your office. As contracts, letters from clients and other vendors, and important faxes are received at your office, file them immediately into the appropriate folder or binder.

3.1.3   People Skills

You can have the know-how to plan an amazing event, but you don't get the chance to show off your talents until you land the job. Party planners need to have excellent interpersonal skills to impress their potential clients. Here's why.

When we have a problem with an air conditioner not working, we can look someone up in the Yellow Pages. They come to your home, they (hopefully) fix your machine, and they leave. However, when we seek a party planner, we are looking for someone who will be responsible for a special event. They will be interacting with the people we have long-term relationships with.

We want to trust a party planner. In some ways, your clients don't just buy your services, they buy you. If they like you, they're more likely to like your proposal and your services. Here are some areas you should work on, starting today.

Building Relationships

When given a choice between two equally competent party planners, clients are going to select the planner they like and trust the most. The best way to come across as likeable and trustworthy is to work on your relationship-building skills. "Clients want to trust the person they are hiring," says Lynn H. Wheatley of Lasting Impressions. "It's a combination of delivering product in a professional manner, and being sensitive to the clients' needs."

To build trust, you need to meet any deadlines that you or your client sets. You should also return phone calls or email messages as soon as possible. There are also organizations that are focused on building interpersonal skills. Traci Romano of The Romano Group Event Planning + Design recommends Toastmasters International which you can learn more about at **www.toastmasters.org**. We also recommend reading Dale Carnegie's classic *How to Win Friends and Influence People*, which tells you how to be likeable by being the kind of person people enjoy.

Listening Skills

Most people think they have excellent listening skills, and in fact, most people are wrong about that. It's especially important for people who provide a specialized service (like party planners do) to be talented listeners.

"You have to learn to read people and really listen to what they are saying," says Bobbie Yarrusso of Creative Event Designs by Bobbie. "If not, you and your client could be on totally different pages as to the expectations of the event. The best advice I can give is that you have to listen to the client and ask questions."

Talk to your client and find out what they envision. Do they want a formal affair? Do they want a traditional event? Do they want a relaxed atmosphere? Do they want the party to have a theme? Before you can help shape things, you need to know exactly what your client's expectations are and find out if they have a clear idea of what they want.

Work on improving your listening skills with you family and friends, who will give you honest feedback about your talent for hearing what they have to say.

Diplomacy

In some cases, your client is going to have a vision for their party that is unrealistic, impractical, or truly horrific. If you feel your client is heading down the wrong path, it is your job to point that out, but only after you hear what they have to say. Then be as tactful as possible when explaining how you believe something could be handled differently.

You may want to let them know you have heard their suggestions and then point out potential pitfalls. You could say, "While that is a good idea, there are some problem areas such as A, B and C. Another way we can handle those things is to…"

Negotiation Skills

Party planners use their talent for negotiation on nearly a daily basis. When you are figuring out what your vendors can provide, a smart party planner knows that just about anything is negotiable. Your ability to get great value and competitive prices for your client will depend on your skills of negotiation.

When you are negotiating with vendors, don't forget to point out the ways you are already compromising. Maybe the venue didn't have the exact time your client wanted. Fine, but that should be worth some complimentary champagne while the guests wait in the lounge.

Remember, you have the upper hand with most suppliers and service providers, who will certainly want your business. Drive a hard (but fair) bargain, and pass treats and savings along to your client. There is always a little room for negotiation.

3.1.4   Creativity

Some people think creativity is an inherent skill, but it can be learned as well. Your clients will have ideas of their own, but they will also rely on your creative ideas to add inspiration to their get-together. They want to host an event that is truly unique — something that is new and exciting to both them and their guests.

Although you can research ideas through magazines, books, or websites for party ideas, you need to be open to the inspiration all around you. When you walk through a store, see a movie, or read a newspaper article, in the back of your mind you will always be thinking "party, party, party." It's true!

"Some of my favorite places for party goods are fabric wholesale stores, dollar stores, Pier One, liquidation wholesalers, and small gift and home décor boutiques. I often find inspiration in items that I see every day, and have a hard time resisting the temptation of buying everything so that I will have it for future events," party planner Kathleen Kellner told us.

To get inspired, try browsing through home and lifestyle magazines, and keep your eye out for the little details — a jar of antique marbles on a table, or a fresh way of displaying a napkin. Keep in mind that there are usually less-expensive ways to recreate a beautiful setting for your clients.

You can subscribe to trade magazines such as Special Events (**www. specialevents.com**) and BizBash New York (**www.bizbash.com**), or check out their online versions listed below. HGTV and Style Network often have design shows, and E! and The Learning Channel (TLC) tend to feature event-oriented shows. Some of the websites listed in section 3.2.1 have specific message boards and advice columns dedicated to creative ideas.

Other people who provide services at events can also be a great source for tips on what other party planners are doing that are popular with their clients and the guests attending the functions.

TIP:　　As someone in the "entertainment business," it is extremely important to stay on the cutting edge. You don't want to be known as the party planner who relies on other people's ideas, so always put your own twist on them.

Here's a final thought from Kathleen Kellner of Eventful Productions: "Quite often the client is the one who gives me the inspiration, whether they realize it or not!" she admits. Be sure to tap into your client's natural creativity as well.

3.2   Event Education

A formal education isn't necessary in the field of party planning, but if you are short on time, there are some effective training programs you can take that will give you a quick boost in the business. You can also set your own course of study using books and websites.

"There are many great event profession organizations that offer education (and networking opportunities) for professionals in all aspects of the event industry," confirms party planner Kathleen Kellner. Here are some options to consider.

3.2.1   Informal Learning

You don't have to wait to get started training to become a party planner. Your informal education can start right now. With the explosion of the Internet, people are now sharing their party-planning ideas with other people around the world.

And since parties are de rigueur in many people's lives, you can also learn a lot from information that is geared towards people who want to plan their own parties. It's time to become a party expert, with the resources listed below.

Websites

The Internet is rich with knowledge on party planning. There are a number of sites that offers tips, news, lists of resources and vendors, and networking opportunities. Here are a few sites that you may find helpful.

Our Favorites

- *Party 411*
  A fantastic resource for themes, etiquette advice, and more. Their message board includes a forum for professional party planners to discuss ideas.
  www.party411.com

- *Party Pop*
  A very useful site for party tips, themes and advice. Use the menu along the right hand side to guide you. The message boards have a lot of "junk messages" on them, but if you are patient you may dig up a few gems. Also includes the afore-mentioned budget calculator.
  www.partypop.com

- *BizBash*
  This website has a terrific section that gives event reports on some of the top events and functions in New York City, Los Angeles, Washington, Florida, and Toronto. Reading these can give you some fresh ideas for your own events. Its section of "Trends & Ideas" also is a valuable resource and a Q&A section offers some great tips as well.
  www.bizbash.com

More Useful Party Planning Resources

- *About.com: Entertaining*
  http://entertaining.about.com

- *Event Planner*
  www.event-planner.com

- *HGTV*
  (Click on "At Home" then "Entertaining")
  www.hgtv.com

- *International Special Events Society*
  www.ises.com

- *Martha Stewart*
  www.marthastewart.com

- *Shindigz*
  www.shindigz.com

- *The Great Event*
  www.thegreatevent.com

Books

Books provide a source of education that you can "complete" at your own pace. Another plus to investing in books is that you will always have them nearby when you need some last-minute inspiration and ideas. There are oodles of books out there about entertaining, although many focus on dining.

These are our top 5 to get you started:

- *Fête Accompli! The Ultimate Guide to Creative Entertaining*
  by Lara Shriftman and Elizabeth Harrison

- *InStyle Parties*
  by the InStyle editorial staff

- *Occasions*
  by Kate Spade

- *Plan a Fabulous Party In No Time*
  by Tamar Love

- *The Party Planner*
  by David Tutera

3.2.2   Short Seminars and Workshops

A number of event associations have yearly conferences where seminars and workshops are given. This type of learning experience can offer specific training in one area of the field, and sharpen up some general skills you will need. Plus you can network with other professionals in your field outside of the classroom setting.

Association conferences offer a wide range of topics generally over a three- or four-day period. These organizations often have local chapters that also host educational opportunities in the form of workshops, seminars, or lectures. Here are some of the better-known event-planning trade shows and conferences, and a brief sampling of what you can expect from them.

Special Event Conference Trade Show

This show, held annually each January in various locations in the U.S., draws approximately 5,000 participants including event planners, wedding planners, caterers, party rental companies, floral designers, decorators, club and banquet managers, and event site companies.

The four-day conference features a number of workshops. Some recent topics include: "Survival Skills for the Event Director," "The Idea Inferno — Hot Event Ideas to Spark Your Development Efforts," and "The Ultimate Checklist Revisited." For information visit **www.thespecialevent show.com**.

ISES Eventworld — An Institute for Professional Development

This is an annual event run by the International Special Events Society (**www.ises.com/education**). The event offers a vast array of educational programs as well opportunities to get hands-on training while allowing you the chance to build contacts and network. This organization has local chapters in the United States, Canada, Europe, Asia, South Africa and Australia.

Each chapter within these countries and continents runs local special events and seminars as well. "I have come to know many of my vendors through the Calgary ISES Chapter. Most of the monthly networking meetings for ISES are held at suppliers' places of business," adds Kathleen Kellner.

BizBash M&C Meeting and Event Style Show

This show recently drew some 3,000 professionals from the Northeastern U.S. Recent topics included "Décor and Design Showcase," "Trends in Lighting and Stage Design," and "Making Sponsorship Succeed." For information visit **www.bizbash.com** (click on "Trade Show" in the "Our Trade Shows & Events" section).

Become Certified in Event Planning

Although you don't have to be certified to be a party planner, it will set you apart from other party planners in your area, and is something you may want to consider. The International Events Society offers the chance to become a Certified Special Events Professional (CSEP). The criteria for earning this certification include education and experience. You must also pass the Certified Special Events Professional (CSEP) Exam. You must be recertified as a CSEP every five years. You can find information about CSEP at **www.ises.com/CSEP**.

3.2.3   Hospitality-Related Courses

Event planning and party planning are related to the hospitality industry, which trains caterers, chefs, and restaurant and hotel managers as well. If you have the money and the desire, a diploma or even some courses in hospitality management will serve you well.

Use your own judgment — if you've never worked in a restaurant or a hotel, or had any experience coordinating an event, you might be a good candidate for formal education. Alternately, you can get some experience working in one of these types of businesses, as we'll explain in the next section.

In a recent online search, we found more than 200 universities and colleges offering hospitality programs. The top-ranked undergraduate hospitality and tourism management program in the United States is at Purdue University, according to two surveys in the *Journal of Hospitality and Tourism Education*. (Visit **www.cfs.purdue.edu/HTM** for more information about Purdue's program.)

There are many other excellent programs throughout the United States, Canada, and overseas. The website of Meeting Professionals International has an extensive list of universities and colleges which offer programs in meeting planning, hospitality and tourism. Many of these educational institutions also offer continuing education and distance learning options or online courses. You can see the list at **www.mpiweb. org/CMS/mpiweb/mpicontent.aspx?id=153**.

There are some additional schools not listed at MPI which you can access from the Convention Industry Council's (CIC) website at **www.conventionindustry.org/resources/industry_resources.htm** (scroll down to "Education and Professional Development").

You can also find lists of hospitality and tourism degree programs at the Hospitality Sales and Marketing Association International (HSMAI) website located at **www.hsmai.org/Resources/degree.cfm**. Another list comes from USNews.com's report on America's Best Colleges 2008. The list is available at **www.usnews.com/usnews/edu/college/majors/brief/major_52-09_brief.php**.

For Canadian programs, including certificate and diploma as well as degree programs, check out SchoolFinder (**www.schoolfinder.com/schools**). Under "Program Search" do a search for event management. You can also try other search terms such as hospitality or tourism.

3.2.4   Continuing Education Classes

Although it can be a lot of fun, don't lose sight of the fact that party planning is still a business. You will need to keep your books, write invoices, meet with clients, log your mileage, file your taxes, advertise your services, and pay your bills.

If you haven't taken any business classes or do not have experience in this area, you may want to look into educational opportunities in this subject. In addition to business classes, many colleges and universities offer a variety of continuing education (also called "extension") classes in subjects that can help make you a better party planner.

Some suggestions are listed below:

- Classes in calligraphy, card-making, or any craft course will help you learn the hand-eye coordination necessary to do up beautiful invitations and centerpieces. These are often offered free by craft stores, or through your community.

- Flower-arranging classes could be very useful to help you decorate for parties, as would any training in interior design.

- Computer design programs (e.g. Adobe InDesign, Quark XPress, and Microsoft Publisher) can give you the necessary skills to do invitations, menus, and even ads for your business on your home computer, saving you and your clients money. These programs even come with tutorials so you can learn them at home.

- Bookkeeping is a necessary skill, and it won't hurt to have some background in this area, even if you plan to hire a professional to keep your books.

- Having a background in business administration under your belt will be very helpful. Look for educational opportunities that offer you the chance to learn about management, marketing, and computer systems.

- If you aren't proficient in computer software such as Microsoft Word, Excel, or PowerPoint, you may want to take a class to learn how to use these programs. They can help you with writing proposals, doing budgets, and making presentations, all of which will be part of your daily work.

- Look for night classes in negotiation tactics, so you can haggle with your vendors and get what you want every time.

3.3 Getting Some Experience

So you have completed your initial education in the field of party planning — whether that means you have read and reread this guide; have taken some classes in the field or related areas; or have done research through books, magazines, and the Internet.

You are ready to get started, but have no actual experience that will convince clients to hire you. What can you do? The easiest way to get your name out there and get some hand-on experience in the field is to start throwing parties, for yourself, for friends and family… any way you can.

You will get hands-on experience picking out invitations, setting up an itinerary, decorating your party site, selecting the entertainment, making a guest list, deciding what theme or mood you want to create, organizing the menu, ordering and/or buying supplies, and working within a budget. Here's how to get started.

3.3.1 Host Your Own Parties

You can start out by hosting your own gatherings for family and friends. They don't all have to be huge blow-outs — you'll get a better variety of experience if you host parties of all shapes and sizes.

This type of party will give you experience in a low- or no-pressure situation. The details of the first event you host shouldn't be overwhelming if you keep it small. You can use a small venue (your living room or dining room) and therefore have a small space to decorate or in which to set a mood. And if you are surrounded by family and friends, you will feel comfortable as you practice your new skills.

After you have mastered the small function, you may want to branch out to include more guests and invest more of your resources. You can practice throwing theme parties, and experiment with menus, decorations, and entertainment. If you're on a budget, look for ways to stretch your dollar. Host an international pot-luck, or host a wine tasting where guests each bring a bottle of their favorite wine.

"It is helpful to host parties," confirms party planner Tracy Romano. "Playing the role of host or hostess requires a great deal of planning and communication skills. Have fun with it! Most [party planning] skills are acquired [this way] — rarely is one adept at all the skills it takes to be a successful party planner."

By giving and organizing your own parties, you also will have the chance to get some honest feedback from your family members and close friends whose opinions you can trust. Perhaps you even may ask them to fill out a quick survey or offer some other form of feedback when the event is over. You can learn what your strengths and weaknesses are, and then you will know which areas you need to brush up on or perhaps even take a class or seminar in at a later date.

Work for a Party-Related Business

There are a number of organizations that work with (and occasionally hire) party planners, and it might be helpful to get some experience working for one of these vendors, even if you not working as the person who actually plans the function.

These types of businesses include caterers, florists, party supply stores, country clubs, convention centers, and hotels. You will be making money while you learn more about your chosen career, and perhaps the opportunity will arise to get in on the planning of a function.

You can also call local event planners in your area and offer to work as an intern or as a free set of hands. You should call a variety of different people and try to get some experience with several established planners to see how different professionals handle different situations and functions. "You may not always be paid for your work, but what you will learn along the way is priceless," says Tracy Romano.

3.3.2   Volunteer Your Services

What can be an even more valuable learning experience than hosting your own event is helping your family or friends host their parties and functions. You can offer your services for free and be their party planner.

Here is where you will get some great experience using your interpersonal skills. You should set up a meeting, however informal, with your "client" and go over your checklist. Cover invitations, the guest list, decorations, party theme, entertainment, the menu and beverages, and all other aspects of the job. This is also a great chance to put your creative skills to the test. You can create the mood and ambiance the client wants.

Listen to what your client wants and what their vision is for the party. Practice staying calm if you disagree with their ideas, and try to guide them to an agreeable solution. Even if they are family or friend, your client's wishes are paramount. You are the leader of the event, but they are the host.

You will get some experience working within a client's budget. These parties will give you the chance to put your business sense to work. Are you getting the best deal possible for your client? Have you managed to stay within a reasonable budget yet respect their wishes for food, beverages, decorations, and entertainment? You might even want to go a step further and write up a mock invoice for your services. If this was a paying client, are you making enough money to justify the time you spent? You can use this as research to set your fees.

Again, use these events to get some honest feedback. Even though these may be non-paying clients, you want them to be happy with their experience. If they like or even love the job you have done, this will give you a tremendous boost in confidence. Ask them for a letter of reference, and tell them to refer you to their friends.

> **TIP:** Don't forget to take pictures of the events you work on for free, and document the theme and all aspects of the coordination. You can put these details together into a portfolio (see section 6.2.3) which you can use to show potential clients.

Once you are comfortable planning your own parties and those of family and friends, you can start volunteering your time, free of charge, to charity organizations or local community groups that want to plan events, but may not have the budget to hire you. "It's a great way to get your name out there," says Lynn Wheatley of Lasting Impressions. "Contact your favorite nonprofits and tell them you're available to assist."

Even if you are doing this as a non-paying job, you will want to do top-quality work. This event may be the biggest bash of the year for the organization or agency you are working for, and you want them to be happy with the event and pleased with your work. There will likely be community and business leaders in attendance at such events, and here is where you can really start to grow your clientele list.

4. Starting Your Own Business

Starting your own party planning business is an exciting challenge. You'll be happy to learn it's also relatively simple and inexpensive. Unlike other businesses that may require hundreds of thousands of dollars in start-up capital, you can start a party planning business out of your home, with only a couple thousand dollars (or a few hundred if you have some of your equipment and supplies already).

In this chapter, we'll look at the various things you'll need to plan for to start up your own business. We'll talk about what your business options are (evaluating the market for your services and choosing a niche), and how to put together a plan of action that will take you from concept to paying client.

Next we get into money matters — figuring out how much starting your business is going to cost you, and where you can go for a loan. We'll walk you through the legal issues of choosing a name and registering your business, getting insurance, and the all-important issue of client contracts.

4.1 Envisioning and Planning

Many entrepreneurs claim that getting started is the hardest part of launching any new business. There's so much to do, so where do you start? Getting over the hump and moving yourself and your party planning business forward can be done by answering a few focused questions:

- What is my business?

- Who are my customers?

- Where do I find my customers?

- What do I want from being a party planner?

This section will provide you with the information and resources that you'll need to respond to these questions, and provide you with the starting points you need to transition into party planning with confidence.

4.1.1 Evaluating the Market

One of the first steps to move your party planning business from the idea stage into the business stage is evaluating the potential market for your services. Basically, you want to determine whether or not there are clients out there who would be interested in using your party planning services.

One effective way for party planners to evaluate their market is an informal survey. Connie Thayer, owner of Party Perfect, told us that after throwing many successful parties at her home over the years, she started to consider party planning as a real career option.

Even though she knew her friends and family loved her parties, Connie still asked herself: Are there really people willing to pay me for throwing parties? To find out, she used the simple, yet highly effective, strategy of an informal phone survey.

"I phoned at least 50 businesses to find out if they had company parties and if they would be interested in a party planner, and my particular services," Thayer recalls.

She discovered that most businesses were interested in her services, providing her with enough confidence to pursue party planning full-time. And after 20 years in the business, the rest is, as they say, history.

TIP: If you decide to use a similar tactic, ask to speak with the individual who is usually responsible for organizing company parties, otherwise you may be speaking to someone who has no idea how much work planning a party can be!

Another survey technique is to ask your friends and neighbors what they do for their children's parties, or any other parties that they throw. Follow up by asking if they would ever consider using a party planner, and how much they would be willing to spend.

You can also ask local merchants who sell party favors and accessories if they get any requests from customers looking for party-planning services. Caterers, hotels and convention centers are also good sources of information about the need for party planners in your location.

Another thing you should do is check to see how many other party planners are already working in your area. A quick glance at the Yellow Pages under "Event Planning," "Parties," or an online search on Party-Pop.com (**www.partypop.com**), the party and event planning database mentioned earlier, will uncover the planners working in your town or city.

If you're feeling adventurous, you can phone these planners and tell them that you're thinking of going into business and are hoping to pick their brain. These people likely won't share client information with you, but they may be willing to share information about the local market and economy, advice on vendors, and even tips on advertising.

Don't panic if your search for planners reveals either what you think are too many planners, or few to none at all, especially if your informal survey results were positive. Many planners means a healthy, competitive market. On the other hand, few planners in your area might just mean that you've hit an untapped market.

While your survey results are a great indicator of a potential market, it may be necessary to acquire some hard numbers to back up the results, especially if you are going to write a business plan.

Information on local demographics, average income, top employers, level of education, and other statistics will confirm that there is both a willingness and ability to pay for party planning services in your area. To find this information, contact your local Better Business Bureau (**www.bbb.org**), Chamber of Commerce (**www.chamberofcommerce. com**), and local governments.

4.1.2   Finding a Niche

A niche is a special area of demand for a product or service. Many party planners choose to specialize in a certain way of providing their services (their "niche") so that they are the experts people think of when they consider hiring someone to plan their party.

You can use your personal talents and interests to inspire your niche, or use your market research to help you identify niche markets where there is current demand. What your niche is has no boundaries.

Here are some of the niche areas that many party planners are having success with right now. You may notice that the niche areas are either focused on the type of parties, specific target markets and interests, or demographics:

- Adult birthday parties
- Adult novelty parties
- Anniversary parties
- Baby showers
- Casino parties
- Children's parties
- Corporate parties
- Entertainer parties
- Graduation parties
- Karaoke parties
- Pre-wedding and wedding parties

- Retirement parties

- Theme parties

Another way party planners can specialize is by focusing on being the best at certain aspects of a party. For example, if you're a good cook, you can be the party planner with the great food. Or if you have a talent, or a knack for finding talent, you can be known as the party planner with great entertainment. Here are some other ideas:

- Great decorations

- Great appetizers

- Best bartending services

- Most elegant/creative table settings

- Best service

- Best theme parties

- Best cakes/desserts

- Best entertainment

- Greatest staff

- Great prices

Note that choosing a niche doesn't mean you can't provide clients with any type of party that they want. It simply means that this is your special focus. The core of your business is still as a party planner, any type of party, any time.

4.1.3   What Services to Offer

As noted in an earlier chapter, party planners offer both complete and partial planning services. Full-service party planners handle every aspect of the party for their clients, from catering to clean up. Clients should not have to make any arrangements other than hiring you. Partial service generally means providing specific party services, and does not include arranging for other vendors (although you should offer referrals).

Party planners who offer full services accomplish this in one of two ways. They either arrange every aspect of the party by dealing directly with contractors, or they take contractors out of the equation by creating and supplying everything themselves, from food to decorations.

In the end, choosing what services to offer really boils down to what your strengths are, and what you want to spend most of your time doing. If you really enjoy decorating, make this a focus of your business. If preparing party foods is your thing, make this a large part of your service.

Consider the following services, and think about whether or not you want to handle them. If you only select a few, you are probably more suited to partial services, or you may rely more heavily on contractors. If you want to run the whole show, full service will be your thing:

- Venue rental

- Catering

- Invitations

- Receiving RSVPs

- Entertainment

- Decorations

- Alcohol and Bartending

- Parking

- Party Theme

- Audio/Visual

Of course, the more services you offer and handle for clients, the more you can charge your clients. But if full-service party planning appears too stressful, and is not why you wanted to get into the business in the first place, don't worry. There are many successful party planners who only offer partial services, and play to their strengths.

"The best advice I would give is to recognize and know your strengths and weaknesses. Know when it is time to bring in other professionals, in areas such as décor, floral, lighting," agrees Kathleen Kellner of Eventful Productions.

Take the example of Eric Welch and Matt Sutherland of Amazing Parties in California. They began as a full-service party planning business, but, as Welch notes, they quickly found that offering partial services based on what they do and liked best was a formula that worked for them.

"At first we were providing everything. We had a checklist of items and services that customers could order. Then we realized that we weren't good at this aspect of the business and didn't enjoy it, so we focused on the entertaining. We still offer clients contacts for rentals and other services, and we try to arrange a discount for them. But we are hired to provide a party centered around entertainment," Welch told us.

It is important to note that no matter how you specialize your party planning services, you must be able to provide clients with a direct line to anything else that they may want for their party. You are, after all, the party planner!

4.1.4 Choosing a Business Name

Choosing a name for your party-planning business can be fun, and there's a lot of room for creativity. There are, however, a few considerations to ensuring that your business name is right for your business, as well as legal.

A good name informs potential clients what business you're in. For example, what good is a name like "Wonders"? It might be wonderful, but at what? Let your clients know that you're in the party business, and include the word "Party," capital P, in your name, or some closely related word, such as event or affair. The word "planner" is another way for your name to say that you're in the party business.

If you can't seem to find a name that you like using one of these words, find a name that hints or implies that you're in the party business. Christine Stieber, an eighteen-year veteran of the party planning business and party planning instructor, chose "The Perfect Day." This name tells clients that a "perfect day" is what you get when you hire her services.

Your business name can also be more specific and reflect a specialization or image, such as these real examples:

- RSVP Party Planners — Denotes elegant parties using the French expression "RSVP"

- Party Painters — You know it's going to be a party and paint will be involved

- New York Party Works — This name establishes location and line of business

The other important aspect of choosing a business name is ensuring that no one else in the industry is using the name, or that you're not violating any trademarks. Start with an informal Internet or Yellow Pages search to eliminate some names right away.

> **TIP:** A trademark also includes how names sound, not just how they look. For example, you might run into trademark issues if you name your business Fantastic Kids Parties, and there's a party planning business in your area named Funtastic Kidz Parties.

Before officially registering your business name, you must conduct formal fictitious names and trademark searches. (The fictitious names database is where non-trademarked business names are listed.) A trademark database lists all registered and trademarked business names.

In the U.S., the essential place to start is with the U.S. Patent and Trademark Office. You can hire a company to do a name search for you, or conduct a free search yourself at **www.uspto.gov/main/trademarks. htm**. In Canada, the default database for name searches is Newly Upgraded Automated Name Search (NUANS) at **www.nuans.com**. There is a $20 charge for each NUANS search.

> **TIP:** Registering your business name is not a necessity for small businesses, but it will prevent others from using your name. It is a requirement, however, if you are incorporating.

Addtional advice on naming your business can be found at **www.nolo. com**. Choose "Starting a Business" under the "Business & Human Resources" tab, then click on "Naming Your Business."

4.2 Your Business Plan

If you are looking for outside financing from a bank or other lending institutions, a business plan is crucial. But even if you don't require bank financing to start your business, writing a business plan can be a big help. It's like mapping out a journey from right now to when you are successful. It's also useful as a type of checklist for keeping track of what you will need to buy, how much money you'll need initially, and how you are going to market your business. Here how you write one.

4.2.1 Parts of a Business Plan

Although the level of detail and complexity will vary for each business plan, the basic structure is always the same. Here's a brief description of the different parts of a business plan to help get you started.

Title Page

A title page is the cover of your document, and should include your company name, address, and area of business if it's not clear. A title page does not have to be a work of art, but it should be professional-looking and include any company logos or designs.

Executive Summary

An executive summary is a condensed version (1 to 2 pages) of the entire business plan. Here's a tip: write your summary last, and just cut and paste the key elements from the rest of your plan.

Business Overview

A description of your business is just that — a description of the business you plan to start and run. The trick is to include the unique and special things about your business so that everyone who reads your business plan will know you're on to something really fabulous.

Management

This section of a business plan illustrates the qualities and expertise that you bring to your party-planning venture, as well as the attributes of anyone you plan to partner with or hire.

Market/Industry Research

This section should include a description of the party planning niche that you're focused on, and should present the research that you used to justify pursuing this market.

Marketing Plan

What strategies will you use to attract clients to your business? This section should include your advertising approaches, marketing budgets, and any sample advertising materials, such as price sheets and brochures, already in the works.

Financial Analysis

The financial analysis portion provides the readers with insight into your current financial position. If you are attempting to borrow money, this is an important section of your business plan. You may want to seek the services of an accountant or management consultant to help you with preparing these figures.

Appendix

Adding an appendix with personal information adds support to your argument that you are in a position to make your party planning business work. Some things found in the appendix are:

- Your resume

- Letters of recommendation

- Business cards and brochures

- Research to back you up

4.2.2   Additional Resources

If you need specific help with any aspect of your business plan, you can get free assistance by contacting the Small Business Development Administration office in your area. Find the office nearest you by calling 1-800-827-5722 or going to their website at **www.sba.gov**. The SBA also has a step-by-step guide to writing business plans online. The Canada

Business Service Centres (CBSC) provides a sample business plan at **http://bsa.canadabusiness.ca** (click on "Preparing a Business Plan" in the list).

Other Resources

- *SCORE "Counselors to America's Small Business"*
  www.score.org

- *Center for Business Planning*
  www.businessplans.org

- *SBA Small Business Planner*
  www.sba.gov/smallbusinessplanner

4.3   Your Start-up Costs

Service businesses like party planning can be started for a minimal cost. In this section we'll look at some of the expenses specific to party planning, as well as general expenses for any business. If your numbers are telling you that you'll need financial assistance, you'll also find a section on financing options.

4.3.1   Expenses to Expect

Just like budgeting for your clients' parties, no one can forecast a start-up budget to the penny. However, having a good understanding of what the costs are of doing business as a party planner will get you a pretty good estimate. You'll find a *Sample Start-up Budget* later in this section.

Most start-up costs fall into four main categories:

- Business

- Office

- Marketing

- Party supplies

No matter how diligent you are about making a start-up budget, there are always some expenses that will be overlooked or that don't fit nicely into any category. For example, you may have to update your wardrobe to include some party outfits, or decide to buy walkie-talkies to communicate with your assistant or staff at a party.

> **TIP:** Don't forget that, as a self-employed entrepreneur, many of the expenses listed below may be eligible for a tax write-off.

Business Expenses

These are the basic "costs of doing business," and include:

- A business license
- Business plan consultants
- Accounting services
- Legal services (e.g. having a lawyer look over your client contracts)
- Business banking fees
- Transportation
- Insurance
- Cell phone
- Mortgage/rent
- Utilities
- Interest on loans/line of credit

> **TIP:** When preparing your budget, keep in mind that any one-time, ongoing and periodic expenses should all be included in your start-up budget to give you an accurate picture for what you need in the first month of business.

Office Expenses

Although much of your work will be out "in the field," there are still administrative tasks to take care of. If you don't already have these items they will, of course, add to your overall costs, but they will also make the business part of party planning that much easier:

- Computer

- Computer software

- Printer

- Digital camera or scanner

- Internet service

- Business phone line/800 number

- Office supplies

- Office furniture

- Answering machine

- Cell phone

Sample Start-Up Budget

Posh Parties by Paula
Start-up Budget

CURRENT CAPITAL	
Cash	$3,000
Line of Credit	$2,000
Total	$5,000

EXPENSES	
Business license	$70
Banking set-up and checks	$100
Initial advertising	$500
Office supplies	$200
Website design	$1,000
Computer	$750
Printer	$500
New clothes	$500
Cell phone	$80
Contingency fund	$300
Total one-time expenses	$4,000

Marketing Expenses

Starting a business is one thing, but you're not in business until the public knows that you're open and operating. To do this, you need to sink some of your start-up capital into marketing your party planning business. Here are some marketing items to consider as part of your start-up expenses:

- Business cards
- Brochures
- Price sheets
- Advertising
- Website (design and updates)

Party Supply Expenses

You may or may not purchase party supplies. In fact, some party planners do not own supplies at all. But if your business focuses on birthday, anniversary, or any other type of small or residential party, you will find that having some frequently used items on hand will pay off:

- Decorations
- Linens
- Centerpieces
- Flatware
- Dinnerware/Glasses
- Costumes and Props

4.3.2   Financing Options

In the sample budget just shown, you'll notice that the planner had a line of credit to help her meet her start-up needs. If you're coming up short in your cash flow, you may want to look to outside funding to start up your business too. This section will look at several options for finding start-up capital, as well as some of the resources that you can turn to for more information.

Banks

Nearly all banks have small business departments that work with entrepreneurs. When approaching a bank for a loan or line of credit, keep in mind that your personal credit and financial history will be closely scrutinized. Start by approaching the bank where you have your personal account, but don't rule out other banks in your city.

Rather than asking for a loan, the best option for a party planning business is usually to obtain a line of credit. A line of credit basically works like a credit card, except that the interest rates are lower. What's more, they're often easier to get approval for than a loan.

Home equity is another option many banks are willing to consider when working with entrepreneurs, so be sure to inform your loan officer if you would be interested in this option.

Loans, lines of credit, and home equity are also available from a credit union. For more information on credit unions and to find one in your area, see the Credit Union National Association (CUNA) website at **www.creditunion.coop** or the Canadian site **www.cucentral.ca**.

Investors or Partners

Investors lend money for businesses, ideas, inventions, and anything that will potentially make money. You may have or be able to attract some investors to put money into your party planning business. Unless you know them well, investors will want to see detailed evidence that your idea is a sound one.

You may also consider partnering with another person to start your party planning business. This is very common in the industry, since there are so many details to handle, and so many diverse skills to possess. Think about anyone you know who might be willing to partner up with you —and of course, put in half the start-up cash.

Family

Don't discount talking to a relative about the possibility of investing in your business. In their book *Fête Accompli*, renowned party planners

Lara Shriftman and Elizabeth Harrison confessed that they started their party planning business with a $5,000 loan from Lara's parents, and began working out of Lara's apartment. They now boast a huge repertoire of A-list clients they have planned events for.

Have a fair interest rate in mind when you approach your family for money. There's also the option of offering shares in the business and the profits, which may appeal to relatives with an entrepreneurial spirit. If you do borrow money from a relative, be sure to draft a written agreement and have each party sign a copy.

4.4 Legal Matters

Even an industry dedicated to fun can't escape paperwork. Whether you're running your party-planning business from a home office or a storefront location, a valid business license, obtained from the city licensing office, is required.

Business licenses are relatively inexpensive, with the average being around $100. You'll also need to obtain insurance, prepare to file your taxes, and have a binding contract ready for your clients to fill out. Here's what needs to be taken care of.

4.4.1 Insurance

There are three must-have policies for protecting your party planning business: liability insurance, property/business insurance, and if you have employees, workers' compensation insurance. Contact an insurance provider for rates and more details. You can often get reduced rates if you work with an insurance company that you're already insured with, such as the agency where you have your car insurance.

> TIP: Talk to the insurance provider about the insurance they offer for individual events, so you can inform your clients about their requirements.

Liability Insurance

Liability insurance is the number-one coverage that you need to protect your party planning business. It is designed to shield you from devastating financial losses that come from clients filing lawsuits claiming that you, or your staff, were negligent in your services or did not deliver what was promised. (Say, in a worst-case scenario, one of your staff burns the venue to the ground.)

It should also protect you from any mishaps or accidents resulting in injury. The minimum coverage that you should consider is $1 million. However, the best way to ensure that your needs are being met is to talk to an insurance agent about the nature of your business.

Business Insurance

Many property or home insurance policies cover home-based businesses as well, but it might be necessary to slightly adjust the policy, which could result in higher premiums. See an insurance agent for details.

There are also small business insurance policies that can provide additional coverage for a portion of your wages in the event that there is an interruption in your business due to unforeseen circumstances, such as a fire that destroys your computer and other tools of your trade. These policies may also have provisions that provide you with loaned equipment until permanent replacements can be provided.

Workers' Compensation Insurance

Most states and all provinces require that small business owners who hire others carry workers' compensation insurance. WCI protects businesses from lost revenues by removing some of the financial burden of having injured or sick employees on the payroll, and protects employees from lost wages as the result of injury or sickness on the job.

If you routinely hire assistants and other service people such as independent wait staff for your parties, these are people being contracted by you, and therefore any claims would come under your WCI coverage. If, however, you partner with a catering firm and they supply the wait staff, the catering company's coverage is used by these employees. Your liability insurance will cover anything that happens as a result of the sub-contracted staff. For more information on WCI, visit **www. workerscompensation.com**.

4.4.2   Taxes

Taxes are an inevitable part of doing business. In both the U.S. and Canada, small businesses are responsible for paying taxes to three levels of government: federal, state/provincial and local. As state, provincial and local tax rules vary (see your local-level governments for details), this section will introduce you to the federal taxes that you'll be responsible for, as well as provide you with some additional resources.

Depending on the type of services and the business structure of your party-planning venture, properly handling your taxes in the U.S. may require that you apply for an Employee Identification Number (EIN), also known as a Federal Tax Identification Number. In Canada, you may require what is known as a Business Number (BN).

With or without one of the above identification numbers, all small businesses in the U.S. are required to file a 1040 form and a Schedule C. Small businesses in Canada running a sole proprietorship will have to fill out both a T1 personal tax form, as well as a business income form, which is the T2124 for a sole proprietorship.

What changes when you transform yourself from an employee to an entrepreneur is that your employer no longer takes responsibility for paying your personal income tax. The responsibility is now yours. To ensure that you're withholding enough taxes from your revenues to keep your head above water at tax time, a good rule of thumb is to always hold back between 25 and 30% of your net income. In Canada, anyone whose business generates more than $30,000 per year is required to register for a Goods and Services Tax (GST) number, and must collect the 7% tax from their clients.

For more information visit the Internal Revenue Service site at **www.irs.gov** or the Canada Revenue Agency site at **www.cra-arc.gc.ca**.

4.4.3   Contracts

The idea of writing a client contract might seem a little intimidating. After all, this is a legally binding document for both you and your clients. However, doing a contract now can save you the services of a lawyer later on, so you might as well protect your interests.

Knowing the basics of what to include in a contract will arm you with enough information to write and present a contract to your clients with confidence. You may still want a lawyer to review a contract after it's been written, just for a second opinion.

So what should be included in a client contract? A client contract establishes in writing:

- What services will be provided
- When the services will be provided
- How the services will provided
- The cost of the services (and when you expect to be paid)
- The client's obligations

As you can see, the content of a contract is information that can and should be established through meetings with the client. Once established, draw up a contract and present it to your client – either in person or through email, fax or mail – for review and signing before beginning work on their party.

On the pages that follow you will find two sample contracts. The first is a *Sample Engagement Letter* you might use with a client planning a relatively simple event. The second is a *Sample Service Agreement* which you could adapt for use with a corporate client or for a major event. It covers a number of additional areas, such as a product/service liability disclaimer so that you cannot be held liable for defects in items you buy or services you subcontract for your clients.

4.5 Franchising

If you are eager to start your own party planning business, but are concerned about the many facets involved in getting everything set up, you may want to consider franchising. Franchising is a business model which allows someone (i.e. you) to run a local business using an established regional or national company or corporation name, logo, products, services, marketing and business systems. The original company is known as the "franchisor" and the company that is granted the right to run its business according to the franchisor's business model is known as the "franchisee."

Sample Engagement Letter

(On Your Letterhead)

[Insert name of Client]

[Insert address of Client]

[Date]

Dear *[Name of client]*,

As promised, I have set out below a description of the services that *[your name/company]* will provide to you.

I will provide the following services:

[Insert description of the services, such as consultations with the client, getting bids from vendors, on-site coordination of the party, etc.]

My fee for the services performed will be as follows:

[Insert rates, amount of deposit, etc.]

If you agree that the foregoing fairly sets out your understanding of our agreement, please sign a copy of this letter in the space indicated below, and return it to me at *[insert address, fax number or e-mail address]*.

Yours sincerely,

[Name]

Agreed and Accepted:

_____

[Insert name of client]

_____

[Date]

Sample Services Agreement

THIS AGREEMENT is made this [date] day of [month], 20__.

BETWEEN
[insert name of your client] (the "Client"); and
[insert your name or your company's name] (the "Party Planner"),
collectively referred to as the "Parties."

The Client wishes to be provided with the Services (defined below) by the Party Planner and the Party Planner agrees to provide the Services to the Client on the terms and conditions of this Agreement.

1.1 Services

The Party Planner shall provide the following services ("Services") to the Client in accordance with the terms and conditions of this Agreement:
[Insert a description of the services here]

1.2 Fees

As consideration for the provision of the Services by the Party Planner, the fees for the provision of the Services are *[insert fees here]* ("Fees").

The Client *[shall/shall not]* pay for the Party Planner's out-of-pocket expenses comprising *[insert here, if agreed]*.

1.3 Payment

The Client agrees to pay the Fees to the Party Planner on the following dates: *[also specify whether the price will be paid in one payment, in installments, or upon completion of specific milestones]*.

The Party Planner shall invoice the Client for the Services that it has provided to the Client *[monthly/at the event/after the event]*. The Client shall pay such invoices *[upon receipt/within 30 days of receipt]* from the Party Planner.

Any charges payable under this Agreement are exclusive of any applicable taxes and such taxes shall be payable by the Client to the Party Planner in addition to all other charges payable hereunder.

1.4 Warranty

The Party Planner represents and warrants that it will perform the Services with reasonable skill and care.

1.5 Limitation of Liability

Subject to the Client's obligation to pay the Fees to the Party Planner, either party's liability arising directly out of its obligations under this Agreement and every applicable part of it shall be limited in aggregate to the Fees.

The Party Planner assumes no liability due to the quality of items or services purchased for the Client.

1.6 Term and Termination

This Agreement shall be effective on the date hereof and shall continue until the date of the event unless terminated sooner. If the Client terminates this agreement for any reason more than 10 days before the scheduled event, the Client will forfeit the deposit paid to the Party Planner and the Client shall reimburse the Party Planner for all outstanding out-of-pocket expenses. If the Client terminates this agreement for any reason within 10 days of the scheduled event, the full fee is payable to the Party Planner and the Client shall reimburse the Party Planner for all outstanding out-of-pocket expenses.

1.7 Relationship of the Parties

The Parties acknowledge and agree that the Services performed by the Party Planner, its employees, sub-contractors, or agents shall be as an independent contractor and that nothing in this Agreement shall be deemed to constitute a partnership, joint venture, or otherwise between the parties.

1.8 Confidentiality

Neither Party will disclose any information of the other which comes into its possession under or in relation to this Agreement and which is of a confidential nature.

1.9 Miscellaneous

The failure of either party to enforce its rights under this Agreement at any time for any period shall not be construed as a waiver of such rights.

If any part, term or provision of this Agreement is held to be illegal or unenforceable neither the validity or enforceability of the remainder of this Agreement shall be affected.

This Agreement constitutes the entire understanding between the Parties relating to the event and supersedes all prior representations, negotiations or understandings with respect to the event.

Neither Party shall be liable for failure to perform any obligation under this Agreement if the failure is caused by any circumstances beyond its reasonable control, including but not limited to acts of God, war, or industrial dispute.

This Agreement shall be governed by the laws of the jurisdiction in which the Client is located.

Agreed by the Parties hereto:

SIGNED by _____

on behalf of _____
[the Client]

SIGNED by _____

on behalf of _____
[the Party Planner]

You have probably bought products and services from many franchises. Burger King, Wendy's and many other fast-food outlets are franchises, as are many others. Industry analysts estimate that franchising companies and their franchisees accounted for $1 trillion in annual U.S. retail sales from 760,000 franchised small businesses in 75 industries so clearly franchises can be very successful business models to start with.

4.5.1   Pros and Cons of Franchising

Often, people who choose to franchise do so because they want to minimize their risk. By working with an established system, franchisees hope to avoid costly mistakes and make a profit more quickly, especially since the business probably already has name recognition, products and marketing concepts that are popular among the public.

Franchises have some unique advantages. Buying a ready-made business means you don't have to agonize over the minute details of a business plan, you do not have to create a logo and letterhead, and the organization of your business is already done. Plus, there is less risk with a ready-made business with a proven track record.

Franchises are good for people who want support running their business. The franchisee may receive assistance with everything from obtaining supplies to setting up record keeping systems. Many franchisors are continuously working to develop better systems and products and you can take advantage of those developments.

Franchisors typically provide a complete business plan for managing and operating the business. The plan provides step-by-step procedures for major aspects of the business and provides a complete matrix for management decisions confronted by its franchisees.

If you choose to franchise, remember that although you own the business you do not own any of the trademarks or business systems. A franchisee must run their business according to the terms of their agreement with the franchisor. In exchange for the security, training, and marketing power of the franchise trademark, you must be willing to give up some of your independence. If you are a person who likes to make most decisions on your own or to chart the course of your business alone, a franchise may not be right for you.

Since someone else is ultimately "in charge," you may be wondering how having a franchise is different than being an employee. In fact, there are significant differences. You have more freedom than an employee; for example, you might choose your own working hours. And you could ultimately earn a lot more money than an employee.

On the other hand, franchisees must pay thousands of dollars up front for the opportunity to work with the business. In addition, you will be required to cover your own operating costs (including the cost of staffing), pay a franchise fee and a percentage of total sales.

4.5.2   Franchise Costs

Entrepreneur Magazine describes a franchise fee as a one-time charge paid to the franchisor "for the privilege of using the business concept, attending their training program, and learning the entire business." Other start-up costs may include the products and services you will actually need to run the business, such as supplies, computer equipment, advertising, etc.

The fees for operation will vary from franchise to franchise, and may rely heavily on location, but expect the franchise fee for a party planning business to be somewhere between $15,000-25,000, with additional start-up costs. The party planning companies we looked at had franchise fees ranging from about $18,000 to $25,000, not including start-up costs (you can read more about these in the next section), although there are other franchises that cost considerably more.

There are a variety of factors involved in determining the initial investment. For example, if you are interested in operating an Andy's Parties franchise, the average total investment will be between $55,000 to almost $100,000 depending on the geographic location and the size of the operation. Most franchise owners obtain financing for their business by providing approximately 35% of the total capital, and then arrange a business loan from a local bank for the balance of the total investment required. None of the franchises we looked at provide any type of financing.

In addition to your initial investment, you can expect to pay the franchisor ongoing royalties, generally on a monthly basis. These royalties are usually calculated as a percentage of your gross monthly sales, and typically range from 2 percent to as much as 10 percent; the exact amount will depend on the company you franchise with. This is the corporation's cut for providing you with their business model and good name.

4.5.3 Choosing a Party Planning Franchise

If you are interested in a franchise, it is important to do your homework on the company you are interested in franchising with. Do your homework and gather all the information you need to make an informed decision. Speak with other people who have invested in the company you are investigating and have an attorney examine the franchisor's contract before you sign anything.

Get some professional opinions on any franchise opportunity you're interested in. Work with an attorney who understands the laws associated with franchising. Also, you may want to work with an accountant to examine your anticipated expenses, your financing needs, and your prospects for achieving your desired level of profitability before you sign any agreement.

Some key points to research:

- The type of experience required to run the franchised business

- Hours and personal commitment necessary to run the business

- Background of the franchisor or corporation

- Success rate of other franchisees in the same system

- Franchising fees to open the franchise

- Initial total investment required to open the franchise

- Cost of operation to continue the right to operate the business as a franchisee

- Any additional fees, products or services you must buy from the franchisor and how they are supplied

For excellent advice on franchising, visit the following websites:

- *Canadian Franchise Association*
  www.cfa.ca

- *Entrepreneur's Franchise Zone*
  www.entrepreneur.com/franchises/index.html

- *Small Business Administration: Buying a Franchise*
  www.sba.gov/starting_business/startup/franchise.html

There are a number of companies offering franchise opportunities in the party planning market. Have a look at the following companies offering franchise opportunities to get an idea of what is involved. Visit their websites for details about their particular franchises.

Note: This list does not represent an endorsement by FabJob or the authors of any of these businesses. They are provided for informational purposes only. Only you know which franchise, if any, is right for you.

Andy's Parties

Website:	**www.andysparties.com**
Details:	Themed parties for children either at Andy's Party Center, client's homes or approved venues; allows franchisees to start as home-based companies first
Franchise fee:	$25,000
Total investment:	$55,000 to $96,000
Royalty fee:	6%
Phone:	(301) 309-2386

Kids Party Planet

Franchise fee:	N/A
Details:	Storefront operation that provides children's (ages 1-12) parties.
Franchise fee:	$25,000
Total investmen:	$82,000 to $117,000
Royalty Fee:	$500 per month
Phone:	(915) 593-1116

Oogles n Googles

Website:	**www.ooglesngoogles.com/franchising.aspx**
Details:	Themed birthday parties for children.
Franchise fee:	$20,000
Total investmen:	$33,400 to $39,700
Royalty fee:	7%
Phone:	(317) 228-9177

Par-T-Perfect

Website:	**www.par-t-perfect.com**
Details:	Provides birthday parties, Christmas parties, weddings, theme parties, etc.
Franchise fee:	$24,500
Total investment:	$35,000 to $96,000
Royalty fee:	6%
Phone:	(604) 947-0274

Plan Ahead Events

Website:	**www.planaheadevents.com**
Details:	Full-service, home-based party and event planning company from small parties to gala events
Franchise fee:	$17,500 to $24,500 (depending on location)
Total investment:	$26,000 to $33,000
Phone:	(800) 466-2812

5. Running Your Business

Once you've got the basics in place, it's time to get ready to start offering your services. This chapter covers choosing an office space and getting the equipment and supplies you need, and how to hire staff when you are ready. It also explores what many party planners cite as the secret of their success: building relationships with local vendors. The chapter concludes with advice on setting your fees and getting paid.

5.1 Setting up Your Space

Here's a look at your space and equipment requirements to get set up and ready to answer that phone when the clients start calling!

5.1.1   Choosing a Location

Party planning is one of those flexible professions in which there are many options for how and where you work. This section will look at the pros and cons of working from home versus renting office or retail space.

The Home Office

Working from home is an option that many party planners choose. The reason is simple: working from home has many advantages. First, it's less expensive. Your home office won't require a deposit for rent or utilities — just fill it with the necessary office equipment and supplies.

A home-business license should be purchased from the local authorities. The cost of this license is minimal, generally between $30 and $100. If you intend to meet frequently with clients at your home, you are considered to be "generating traffic," and it may cost you a bit more.

A home office also provides you with several tax deductions. For example, a portion of your mortgage or rent, based on the square footage being used for your office, can be deducted. As well, a portion of items and services used for your business, such as your phone, Internet, computer and office furniture purchases, can be deducted at tax time.

> **TIP:** In order for your home office to qualify as a tax write-off, your office must be a physically separate space, such as a spare bedroom or a cordoned-off portion of your basement.

Even a room in a basement or at a parent's house is enough for you to sit down and be creative, advises Jennifer R. Rosciti of Dolce Event Productions. There you can store décor that you have, hang ideas on the walls, and keep filing cabinets filled with information about vendors and clients.

What can be a problem for party planners working from home is a lack of space. When party planners own several of the party supplies that they use such as tables, party favors and dishes, this requires storage space. Make sure the space you have in mind will leave you some room to move and think.

An Off-Site Space

For those who don't like the idea of working from home, party planning is also a business that can be run from a rented, leased, or purchased office space.

An office space is ideal for those party planners who like to meet clients on their own turf, as well as those who need extra space to house party supplies, party furniture, and employees. Another advantage of an office space is that it offers a type of free advertising. With an office space in a high-traffic location, your party planning business gets exposure that a home office will not.

The primary disadvantage of an office space is of course paying rent, utilities and taxes. As well, some party planners will argue that office space is simply not necessary for those in the business, particularly those just starting out.

Retail space is another consideration, but it's really only advantageous if you will make retail sales and rentals of party supplies part of the business. The high cost of retail space can be prohibitive for many just starting out in the business. However, if you can afford the monthly overhead, selling and renting party supplies can be an excellent complement to your party-planning business.

A Permanent Party Site

A permanent party site is a rented, leased or owned space that is legally designated for commercial use as a gathering space. As the on-site party planner, you are able to provide the location for the party, as well as all the party services.

This concept is especially popular with people who plan theme parties or children's parties, since you don't have to set up and take down complex equipment or decorations after every event… although you do have to clean up! Like a retail space, the cost of this can be prohibitive. But it can also add to the overall value of your party planning business if you have a ready-made venue for each event.

5.1.2   Equipment and Supplies

Although you don't need much to start a party planning business, there are some key pieces of equipment and certain supplies you'll want to have on hand to your job.

> **TIP:** This section does not cover party supplies you may accumulate. Section 5.3.6 will explain what party-related supplies and props you may wish to keep on hand.

Computer

No business can function without a computer, and party planning is no exception. However, it's not necessary to have the top-of-the-line model and spend thousands to get a computer that will meet your needs. Some of the minimum requirements and items to look for when purchasing a new or used computer include:

- Monitor — 15" - 19"

- Processor — At least a Pentium III or 4, running at a speed of no less than 1.4 GHz

- Hard drive — A minimum of 60 GB (Gigabytes) in size

- RAM (Random Access Memory) — 256 MB (Megabyte) minimum

- NIC (Network Interface Card)

- Sound card

- Video card

- CD-ROM/CD-RW — Allows CDs to be played and burned

Other accessories that you might consider include:

- Scanner

- Digital camera

- Surge protector

The above specifications are applicable to both desktop and laptop computers. Deciding between buying a desktop and laptop is really dependent on if you think you would need a portable computer.

If you want to make PowerPoint presentations to your clients or at your parties, having the laptop would be a help. Some drawbacks of laptops include limited battery time, an odd placement of the keyboard, and learning to use a touchpad mouse.

Printer

Since printers don't come standard with a computer, you have some choice as to what to buy. Rest assured that you will need a printer as a party planner — there are contracts to sign, proposals to present, and to-do lists to generate, just as a part of everyday business.

Before you buy a printer, think about what services you want to offer as a party planner. If you want to be able to print nice envelopes, invitations, place cards, and so on for your clients, a laser printer is a better option than an inkjet. They are more expensive, but it gives a nicer look, and you won't be refilling ink cartridges once a week.

Another option when buying a printer is to purchase an all-in-one printer that includes a printer, fax machine, scanner, and photocopier. This type of unit gives you greater functionality and can save you a lot of money over purchasing these items as stand-alone equipment. Prices have dropped considerably in recent years, and you should be able to buy a brand new all-in-one printer for less than $200.

Computer Software

The Microsoft Office Suite (version 2000 and better) will meet most party planners' software needs. This suite includes Word, Excel, Outlook and PowerPoint, among others, and will fulfill all your word processing, database and email demands.

While the MS suite is good "all-purpose" software, there are other companies that build software focused on specific functions, such as accounting, database organization, and event/party planning.

Business Accounting

One of the most popular, reliable and easy-to-use bookkeeping software is Quicken. This software will help you keep track of your finances, and preparing professional looking graphs and charts is a snap. This package will cost around $100, and online technical support is available. You can buy the software online at http://**quicken.intuit.com**.

Microsoft is also in the business-niche software market with their Money Plus Home & Business, and it is getting excellent reviews. This package starts at around $60. You can download a free 60-day trial version at their website at **www.microsoft.com/money/freetrial_Homeand Business.mspx**.

Contact Database

While in the beginning you might find keeping contact names, numbers and business information an easy enough task, there may come a time when you need a contact management program.

FileMaker Pro (**www.filemaker.com/products/fmp**) has been king of the database world for some time because it's effective and user-friendly, and data from Excel and other software files can be dragged and dropped into the program. It's also reasonably priced at about $299. Another option is Sage Software's ACT! This software also helps you keep track of customer contacts, and is slightly cheaper than FileMaker: about $230. Visit the ACT! website at **www.act.com** to learn more.

One bit of technology Paula Lundgren of Brainstorm Creative Business Services says she finds indispensable is CardScan (**www.cardscan. com**). The device scans business cards into your computer, without you typing it in. "You do have to verify the information for accuracy, but it means you don't have to enter each card individually," she says. "The database also syncs with Microsoft Outlook."

Party Planning Software

As the name implies, party and event planning software was created with the profession and those in it in mind. Although most of this software is said to be for event planners, many of the functions of an event planner and party planner are the same, so it will suit your purposes as well.

One such program is EventPro (**www.eventpro.net**). This software includes a booking wizard, venue management tool, and staff coordination tool, among other features. This may not be software that you'll need right away, but it might be something to consider for the future. Other options include B'nai Mitzvah Party Planning Software (**www. castlecomputer.com/products_bm.php**) and Insight Direct Service CEO (**www.insightdirect.com/event-planning-software**).

If you are not yet able to afford event planning software or not sure you would use it, try a free online service like EZEventPlanner.com (**www. ezeventplanner.com**), which includes task tracking, email reminders, timetables and an online storage site.

Office Furniture

You will require a few essential pieces of office furniture to make your working space comfortable and productive:

- Desk
- Printer table
- File cabinet
- Office chair(s)
- Guest chairs
- Bookshelves

Office Supplies

Most new entrepreneurs are amazed at the amount of office supplies that they use every day. You don't notice as much when your company buys it for you! Here are the basics — you may find that you pick up other helpful supplies to suit your organizational system as you go along:

- Accordion folders
- Calendar
- Day timer

- Envelopes (various sizes)

- Manila folders

- Notepads

- Paper

- Paper clips

- Pens/pencils

- Printer cartridges

- Stamps

Phone and Answering Machine

Party planners spend a lot of time on the phone. You might appreciate having more than one phone line, especially if you are thinking about hiring staff or partnering with another planner. A cell phone is a vital piece of your equipment, and may suffice in lieu of an extra line. Get call waiting if it is available in your area so that clients' calls always get through.

By all means, use an answering system to get your messages. Be sure not to let your box overfill so callers are turned away — this sends a "message" back that says you don't take care of business. Write a script for a friendly message. If you want to have a friend with a nice voice record it, that's an option, too.

EXAMPLE #1:
"You've reached Penny's Parties With Pizzazz. Sorry we can't come to the phone, but if you'll please leave your name, number and a detailed message, we'll get back to you within a day. Thanks for calling. Have a great day!"

EXAMPLE #2:
"You've reached Penny's Parties With Pizzazz, your headquarters for the perfect event. Please leave your name, number and a detailed message, and we'll be delighted to get back to you within a day. We're looking forward to talking you!"

Party Production Box

Party planner Kathleen Kellner of Eventful Productions in Calgary, Alberta was kind enough to share with us the top-secret contents of what she calls her "Production Box." These are the onside tools she takes with her to the events she coordinates, so she is ready to solve any challenge and prevent any disaster for her clients. On the next two pages you'll see what's in the box, so you can start thinking about stocking yours.

What's in a Party Production Box?

Toolbox

❑	Bungee cords (4)	❑	Nails/screws
❑	Craft wire	❑	Pliers
❑	Crazy glue	❑	Rope
❑	Double-sided tape	❑	Scotch tape
❑	Duct tape	❑	Screwdriver
❑	Exacto knife	❑	Spray adhesive
❑	Extension cords	❑	Staple gun
❑	Gloves	❑	String
❑	Hammer	❑	Twine
❑	Hot glue gun/glue	❑	Velcro strips
❑	Lock and key	❑	White glue
❑	Masking tape	❑	Zip cords

Communication

❑	Cell phone/charger	❑	Phone book
❑	Extra battery packs	❑	Two-way radios

Business

❑	Business cards and brochures	❑	Contracts/order forms
❑	Camera	❑	Copies of event agenda
❑	Check book		

Stationery

❏	2 & 3 hole punches	❏	Felt pens (red/black)
❏	Binder	❏	Large Acco clips
❏	Blank CDs	❏	Letterhead
❏	Blank paper (white & color)	❏	Paper clips
❏	Calculator	❏	Pens/pencils
❏	Clipboard	❏	Push pins
❏	Dry erase pens	❏	Scissors (4 pair)
❏	Elastics	❏	Stapler/staples
❏	Envelopes (med & large)	❏	White board

Personal Care

❏	Feminine hygiene products	❏	Nylons
❏	Hair spray	❏	Sewing kit
❏	Lint brush	❏	Shout stain remover pads
❏	Lip balm	❏	Socks
❏	Meal replacement bars	❏	Static Guard
❏	Nail polish remover	❏	Water

First Aid

❏	Antibacterial cream	❏	Pain reliever
❏	Band aids	❏	Rubbing alcohol
❏	Disposable rubber gloves	❏	Safety glasses
❏	Gauze pads	❏	Thermal blanket
❏	Imodium	❏	Throat lozenges
❏	Medical tape		

Miscellaneous

❏	Corkscrew/opener	❏	Paper towels
❏	Drop sheets	❏	Towels/rags
❏	Garbage bags	❏	Windex cleaner
❏	Moving blankets		

5.2 Hiring Staff

Party planning can certainly be a one-person business, but sometimes there is too much going on for one person to handle. This section looks at the difference between contractors and employees, as well as what skills to look for in potential help, and how to arrange payment, so you'll be set to hire when you are ready.

5.2.1 Contractors vs. Employees

When you need help, you have to decide whether to hire a contractor, or take on an employee as part of your staff. First, you need to know what the difference is between a contractor and an employee. Secondly, you need to know what your obligations are to both as the employer. Here is some information to help you make the right decision for you.

The IRS defines a contractor as an individual who is responsible for paying his or her own income tax and other deductions such as Social Security. In Canada, it's defined as those who pay their own taxes and Employment Insurance.

What also defines a contractor is that you only have the right to control the end result of this person's work, not how they do the work. For example, if you contract someone to cater and serve a party, you have the right to determine what and how much will be served. You don't, however, have the right to tell them where to buy their ingredients, or how and where to cook the meal.

On the other hand, the IRS defines an employee as someone for whom the employer takes the responsibility to hold back taxes and other deductions. An employee is also eligible for benefits.

Hiring contractors allows for more freedom to choose whom you want to work with from party to party, and there's less paperwork involved. A binding contract that states what is expected and what will be paid is necessary to protect both parties.

Choosing to hire an employee over a contractor does increase your obligations and paperwork, but it also provides you with a reliable person that cares about and can grow with the business.

The Skills to Look For

When you find yourself in need of help, knowing what to look for is half of the battle. While there are several specific skills that party planners might hire someone for, many professionals in the industry insist that there are some overall skills to look for when hiring staff, particularly when hiring an employee.

Organization Skills

Party planning is all about logistics. There's a lot going on, and a lot of detail to attend to, so good organizational skills should be the number-one skill to look for when interviewing prospective employees.

Interpersonal Skills

Many people working for you, such as servers and entertainers, won't just be working behind the scenes; they'll be interacting with guests at the party. Therefore, interpersonal skills, defined essentially as the ability to communicate, are a must.

Problem-Solving Skills

No matter how diligent you are about planning a party, there's always a chance that something will go wrong. So it's imperative that those you hire can maintain their composure and find ways to resolve any issues that arise.

Math Skills

While party planning is certainly a creative business, it's also a business of numbers. How many meals, glasses and plates do you need? How much should we charge per head? Good math skills, particularly for an assistant position, are a must.

Listening Skills

These are a necessity for employees to understand instructions from both you and the client.

Positive Attitude

Professional planners can't state enough the importance of having upbeat, friendly staff. After all, who wants a "wet blanket" at their party?

5.2.2   Conducting Interviews

If you're going to hire help, it's important to know a few basics about conducting interviews. This will help you to properly assess potential contractors and employees and subsequently hire the best person for the job.

Interviewing Potential Employees

Interviewing potential employees should be done in person, and should be done only after receiving and assessing the individual's resume.

Here are some questions that will help you determine whether or not an interviewee is right for your party planning business. As you'll see, your interview questions should include a combination of open-ended questions that assess personality, and work-related questions that assess the individual's job knowledge:

- Tell me what you think this job will entail.
- What does customer service mean to you?
- Describe a conflict at a previous job. How did you resolve it?
- Tell me about some previous parties that you've worked at.
- What makes a successful party?
- How long have you been in the industry?
- Do you have any references?

The other thing to keep in mind is that there are some questions you are not legally allowed to ask. Illegal questions are generally personal questions in which the answers could lead to employer discrimination. These are questions about marital status, religion and age.

You can find good advice on hiring employees at Nolo.com (**www. nolo.com**). Click on "Human Resources" under the "Business & Human Resources" tab.

Interviewing Contractors

Interviewing contractors is slightly different from a "job interview." The contractor, such as a caterer, is presumably already an expert or has some experience in their field. Therefore, your job in this interview is to confirm their claims.

Have a list of questions that focus on determining the company's philosophy, experience, and ability to perform the tasks that you're looking for them to fulfill. This initial interview can be done over the phone; however, it's good business practice to visit the contractor in person before making a decision.

You'll find a lot more information about building relationships with contractors in the next chapter of this book, but here are a few questions to help get you started:

- How long have you been in business?

- What is your business philosophy?

- Where do you recruit your employees?

- What size events can you manage?

- What do you charge?

- Who were your last few clients?

- Do you have insurance?

- Do you have references and contact numbers?

Your reputation is a huge part of the referral equation, which is why you need to take those who you work with very seriously. Do you hire teens to help with clean up? Make sure they dress, act and talk respectfully. Do you have a vendor who has disappointed a client by failing to follow through? Reconsider working with them, because further failures will reflect on you.

5.2.3   What to Pay

All staff you hire for your party planning business are entitled to be paid the minimum wage as designated by each state and province. In some states and provinces, there is a separate minimum wage for servers, which is often below the average because they receive tips.

What you pay staff should take into account their level of responsibility. For example, if you hire an assistant who works directly with clients and is present at parties overseeing that the function runs smoothly, then this employee has taken on a high level of responsibility by directly representing your business, and should be paid market-level wages.

Paying a permanent employee of your party planning business can be done in a couple of different ways. The first is to pay by the hour, which is often the best scenario for employees such as wait staff. The second is to pay a percentage of the total profits. For example, if you earn 10% of a $10,000 party ($1,000), you may offer your assistant 2% of the 10%, or $200 for the party. This works well for assistants who are also involved in generating business.

Permanent employees do not have to be paid immediately following the party, because they are on the payroll and can be paid in predetermined intervals, such as bi-weekly. Physically getting money earned by employees to them can be done with cash, check or through direct deposit into their bank accounts. This last option comes with a surcharge from the bank. On the other hand, unless otherwise stated in a contract, contractors must be paid on or before the day that their services are provided.

When hiring contractors, they will more often than not have established prices for their products or services. This doesn't mean, however, that there isn't room to negotiate. For example, a bar service provider may charge $150 for one bartender to work five hours, but you could get two bartenders (and better service) for $250, a savings of $50.

5.2.4 Training

If you do have the opportunity to train employees, here are a few general tips that will provide you with a uniformly professional staff.

Business Knowledge

Any staff you hire should be briefed on your party planning business, and should be able to answer questions such as how long you've been in business, general prices, services offered, and contact information.

Table Settings

Every employee working for you should know how to properly set a table. They could be called to perform this function at a moment's notice.

The Art of Decoration

You will want to train employees on what "professionally decorated" means to you. And nothing is too small to mention. Things such as at what angle to hang banners, lighting and centerpieces, even how you like to drape tablecloths, should be demonstrated to each new employee.

Handling Complaints

Train all employees on what you want them to do when faced with complaints. Help employees recognize problems that can be dealt with on the spot, such as cold soup (just bring the guest another one).

Customer Service

Tell employees what customer service means to you, and train them in ways that will help them reach your vision each time they deal with a guest or client.

Serving

Even if you don't hire someone as a server, there's always a chance of being thrust into performing this function if you are short-staffed.

5.3 Working with Vendors and Suppliers

If you asked 100 party planners to name the secret of their success, the one consistent answer would be having a network of reliable vendors and suppliers. You can have a million great party ideas, but you need the right venues, services, provisions and party supplies to bring your ideas to life.

As a party planner you are often in a position to find, choose and secure – with the client's money – the products and services for the party. What they do and deliver reflects directly on your judgment and abilities as a party planner.

For the purposes of this book, we'll refer to service providers generally as vendors, and product providers as suppliers. This chapter provides the inside track on ways to find and build good working relationships with vendors and suppliers, as well as ways to ensure that you're getting the right company, product or person for the job.

5.3.1   Types of Vendors/Suppliers

The types of vendors and suppliers you will use will depend on how many aspects of a party you facilitate yourself, and how many you contract out to vendors, as well as the types of parties you plan.

Here are some of the main contacts you will need to make to establish yourself as a party planner. Depending on the type of parties you specialize in, you may add on to this list:

- Audio/video service
- Bakers

- Balloon services

- Bartenders

- Caterers

- Chemical vendors (CO2, helium)

- Child-care service providers

- Costume rental companies

- Emergency repair services

- Entertainers

- Florists

- Furniture rental/sales

- Gift basket providers

- Graphic artists

- Hardware stores

- Hotel planners/managers

- Ice houses

- Insurance companies/brokers

- Interior designers/decorators

- Janitorial/cleaning services

- Lawyers

- License/permit authorities

- Lighting designers

- Limousine services

- Linen suppliers/cleaners

- Liquor wholesalers, retailers

- Messenger services

- Musicians

- Novelty companies

- Office supply stores

- On-call medical services

- Party favor makers

- Party retailers

- Photocopy shops

- Photographers

- Pool/hot tub services

- Portable toilet suppliers

- Printers

- Publicists

- Security services

- Sign/banner companies

- Speakers' bureaus

- Specialty foods suppliers

- Stationery stores

- Sports equipment

- Temporary-help services

- Tent/canopy services

- Ticket services

- Truck/trailer rentals

- Valet parking services

- Videographers

- Wait staff

You might be surprised at the length of the above list. While you will not need every type of vendor for every party, the point is to have the contacts in place when you need them, as you'll read in the rest of this section.

5.3.2   Finding Party Vendors/Suppliers

The time for you to find and cultivate vendor/supplier resources is not after you get a paying client, but before that — even before you open for business, in fact. You won't have time to be making new vendor discoveries when you're busy planning a party.

By the time you start networking and negotiating with clients, you should have a solid list of vendors in place. You should ideally be positioned to make deals, or have at minimum a general idea of what they can and can't offer, what they charge, and how they work.

Finding vendors who can supply what you need for a party may seem as simple as a glance through the Yellow Pages, trade magazines, or an Internet search of service-provider websites. But that is far from the whole story. Assembling a list of vendors on whom you can rely is a process of research, discovery, networking, and sometimes strategic wining and dining. "Networking is very important, not just for new clients, but to get to know suppliers and to be known in the industry," confirms party planner Kathleen Kellner.

Sources of Vendor/Supplier Information

The Yellow Pages and other directories are of course excellent sources, as is the local Chamber of Commerce and Better Business Bureau. But you don't have to let your search begin and end with these sources, as they will often have duplicate listings and the same entries each year. A fairly new and excellent resource is the online searchable database PartyPop.com (**www.partypop.com**). This site has thousands of listings of vendors and suppliers (across the United States and parts of Canada) that sell products and services dedicated to the party industry.

For an approach that can pay off with finding the best vendors, be inquisitive. Constantly ask people where they bought items that you think you could use at your parties. At the end of your meal, speak to the manager of a restaurant that you enjoyed dining at about their private party options.

If you go to a club or meeting that is serving a catered lunch and you enjoy the food, find out who the caterer is and get their number. A friend has a nice arrangement of flowers on her kitchen table — which flower shop is it from, and what is the name of the florist?

TIP: Whenever you meet with vendors or suppliers, ask which other companies they frequently work with and can recommend, so you can continue to build up your list.

Don't stop at one contact for each service or supply. Ideally, you want multiple vendor options to accommodate bigger events and diverse tastes. Even in a big city, you may not be able to rent 1,000 chairs locally if those chairs have been committed to another event on the day yours is scheduled. If you know more than one chair vendor, you can just move on to the next one.

Your Vendor Database

In the course of looking for vendors, you should be compiling a database at the same time. Gather and store vendor information systematically. Use a database program to enter the basic contact information so you can retrieve it easily.

What should this database or contact list include? It should include everything from contact information and products, to prices and availability. There should be at least one field available for miscellaneous notes — details about vendor personalities or "to do" reminders. Below is a *Sample Matrix* to give you an idea of what your database will look like.

Sample Matrix

Vendor Information	Contact Person	Products/ Services	Quality	Availability	References	Notes
Perfect Party Rental 1818 Party Place 555-5555 Open 9 – 9 Mon. – Sat.	Rhonda Minten, Manager	Party supplies, tents, dinnerware, tables and chairs	Medium to high-end products	Has at least two sets of all major items, must book two weeks in advance	Nellie's Catering 555-5555 Wild Planners 555-5555	Very eager to help; friendly; Will follow up with R. in 2 weeks
The Party Store 2565 Fun Blvd. Open 9 – 9 7 days a week	Chris Holman, owner	Costumes, table linens, catering supplies	Low to medium end products	Limited selection, requires 3 weeks notice for large items	Dave Thomas 555-5555 Hotel Party 555-5555	Hard to get ahold of — no answering machine and don't always answer phone

---

Finding "Hard-to-Find" Items

If your client is looking for unusual or hard to find items to complement their party theme, you might want to try the Thomas Register, North America's industrial-strength version of the Yellow Pages. The listings are narrowly defined by highly specialized lines of business. Under musical instruments, for example, you can find some 90 companies that manufacture instrument cases and a dozen or so that make organ and piano felt. You can find the Thomas Register online at **www.thomasnet.com**.

5.3.3 Evaluating Vendor/Suppliers

While identifying what and whom you need is one thing, finding the vendors that can deliver is another. The best vendors are those who meet deadlines, keep promises about quality, and who are fair and honest about money.

Christine Stieber, owner of The Perfect Day, agrees that hiring the right vendors can be a challenge, and that they can make all the difference between a good party and a fab party. In fact, it's a point that Stieber continually stresses with her students at Cal Poly Pamona, where she teaches classes in event management.

"I tell my students that the hardest part of my job, and the hardest part of their job, will be choosing and hiring vendors. Why? Simply because they're so important to the success of your parties," she told us.

Before hiring a vendor, Stieber follows a six-step procedure for gathering information and ensuring that she's getting the right vendors, which she was kind enough to share.

1. Contact Supplier by Phone

Suppliers are always happy to hear from anyone with potential business, so don't hesitate to call, learn a bit about them, and make arrangements to meet. However the purpose of the call is to receive more than a happy greeting; you're calling them to gain a first impression of their professionalism and personality.

2. Request Business Information

Ask vendors that you're interested in to send you any brochures or pamphlets that they have about their business. This will give you answers to questions that you may forget to ask, but it also demonstrates a vendor's willingness to do business, as well as professionalism.

3. Meet at the Supplier's Place of Business

Nothing gives you a better indication of the type of business that a proprietor is running than seeing first hand how the operation is run. Some suppliers that you approach will know what party planners do, others will not. Tell them everything about your business, the parties that you've thrown or will be throwing, and why you need their services. The whole idea is to provide them with insight into your business, and don't be afraid to discuss some of the challenges that you face. Chances are, they've faced the same problems and will have some helpful suggestions.

4. Sample the Supplier's Products

Don't take a supplier or friend's vouch that a product or service is good. Ask to sample anything and everything that you may use for your clients. If it's impossible to physically get to a supplier, many out-of-town, and even local, suppliers are happy to deliver samples to your home or business. Just imagine the nightmare scenarios that could arise from not sampling the hors d'oeuvres, or viewing the glassware — think pigs-in-a-blanket and plastic wine glasses.

5. See the Supplier in Action

If possible, ask the supplier if you can visit them while they're working. For example, if they're catering a lunch one weekend, ask if you can drop by. This is the best way to gauge their professionalism, and for you to assess how the guests are responding to their products and services — invaluable insight.

6. Ask For (and Call) Three References

Unless a supplier has just opened their doors, they should be able to provide you with work-related references. It's not enough to just have reference phone numbers; you have to use them. Call all three references and find out how satisfied they were with the supplier's services.

You might also want to check out companies' status with the Better Business Bureau; BBB membership is no absolute guarantee of integrity, but the more information you have, the better. Check into the Internet sites of these companies. Knowledge about how they project a public image is also important.

Buying From Online Vendors and Suppliers

Like nearly everything else, party suppliers can be found and purchased online. The obvious disadvantage of buying online is not being able to see the product firsthand before making a purchase. The best ways to protect yourself from buying products that are not what you expected are:

- Request a free sample beforehand

- Ensure that the company has a return policy

- Ask for referrals from satisfied clients

There are several online party suppliers that operate strictly on the Internet, or have an online presence in addition to their retail or warehouse location. Keep in mind that the Internet business is primarily done using credit cards, and that shipping costs can quickly add up.

Internet sites also provide you with the chance to find unique products that no other planner in your city will have access to. There are many online party suppliers to choose from. Here are a few:

- *Party Supplies Hut*
  http://partysupplieshut.com

- *PartyCheap.com*
  www.partycheap.com

- *PartySolver.com*
  www.partysolver.com

- *Kipp Brothers*
  www.kipptoys.com

5.3.4   Visiting Party Venues

Great party locations are everywhere. It just requires a bit of imagination and know-how to find the right one. One of the first places to start looking is in the Yellow Pages under headings such as conventions, halls and party supplies. Another approach is to pick venues that you think would be great places to hold a party, and contact them to see if they do in fact have party services.

You'd be surprised at the diverse range of venues that hold party services, but use only word-of-mouth advertising. Here are some ideas for party venues found in cities throughout North America. Use your imagination and knowledge of your city to add to your list:

- Art galleries

- Bars and pubs

- Conservatories

- Ferries/riverboats

- Gardens

- Historic houses/manors

- Museums

- Retail stores

- University/college facilities

- Vineyards

- Zoos

While the above list has some great venue ideas, don't think that you have to limit yourself to well-known venues. For example, if you were on a Sunday drive and saw a country ranch with a great barn that would be perfect for a western party, approach the owners and explain what it is you'd like to do, and how much they could earn. If they say yes, you've helped your client have a one-of-a-kind party.

Once you have some venues in mind, it's important to visit the venue in person. Betsie Trammel of P3 Professional Party Planning says that she likes to visit a venue in person not only for all of the practical reasons, but to get a sense of the ambiance of a room. This includes things such as lighting, décor, flooring, art and theme.

"Many venues have everything you need to have a party. But I really think that it's the ambience of the room – how it feels, not just how it looks – that makes a great party location," she explains.

> TIP: Another key reason to view a venue in person is to meet face-to-face with the manager and start to build a relationship, as we'll explain in the next section.

To keep track of the venues that you inspect it's important to take notes. One of the best ways to keep notes, and start a permanent list of venues, is to create a checklist that you can fill in while you're at the venue, and input into your computer when you return to the office.

You can use the *Sample Site Survey Sheet* (from the *FabJob Guide to Become an Event Planner*) on the next page to evaluate a venue, and keep on file. You can make copies for each site you evaluate. You may want to clip a few digital photos or a brochure to the form to jog your memory, and so the client can get a sense of the ambiance as well.

5.3.5   Building Effective Relationships

There is a "small-town" aspect to networking with prospective vendors. When relationships are with people they trust, they are more likely to be flexible with terms and more accommodating of emergency requests. This is simply human nature.

Connie Thayer, owner of Party Perfect, says that most suppliers are willing to work with you and help you get through issues, particularly after you get to know them and start generating business for them.

Thayer says that she's built up her relationship with one particular supplier to such a comfort level that when she had an urgent need for a few hundred champagne glasses, they delivered and accepted payment at a later date. (With this said, in most cases a supplier will need "up-front" money from you or your client in order to provide their services.)

Sample Site Survey Sheet

Venue:		
Address:		
Contact Name:		
Title:		
Phone Number:	Cell Phone:	
Fax:	Email:	
Website:		
Seating capacity:		
Number of rooms:		
Floor plans available:		
Parking spaces:	*Number:*	*Charge:*
On Site Catering:		
Staff:		
Washrooms:	*Number:*	*Condition:*
Handicapped facilities:		
Washrooms:	*Parking:*	*Ramps:*
Deposit:		
Cancellation policy:		
Audiovisual capabilities:		
Linens:		
Table decorations:		
Outdoor facilities:		
Gratuities:		
Janitorial service included:		
Kitchen:		
Professional or Home style Appliances:		
Bar:		
Portable or Static:		
Lighting:		
Natural:	*Artificial:*	
Cleanliness:		

Many suppliers will offer a discount for party planners they know and trust, although discounts are generally only offered after you've had a few dealings with them and proven your professionalism.

One approach is to bargain for a discount based on multiple orders. An example might be to ask if you could negotiate a 10% discount if you purchase or rent the centerpieces to match the china.

Another option is to offer, with your client's permission, advertising space for the supplier at the party in exchange for a discount. This can be something as simple as business cards or a small sign being placed at the buffet table.

In the end, the working relationship that party planners have with suppliers may be a lot of work, but it is necessary and can be rewarding and beneficial.

Here are some more tips to help you build good vendor relationships. You can also review to the relationship-building information in section 3.1.3 of this guide:

- Make an effort to remember the names not only of owners and managers but also support staff who work for them. That will come back to you in cooperation and service later.

- Remember that there may be room for negotiation on prices. If you bring two parties a year to Hotel Honeymoon, you will probably be billed for the going rate. If you bring eleven parties a year, that's a different story.

- Don't steal ideas from your vendors and then not work with them. With elaborate designs and themes being so important to the success of parties, personal creativity is on the line. Creative people want to protect their brainchild whether they get the gig or not. Be respectful of this to win vendors' trust.

- Doing business with integrity is the best thing you can do to earn vendor loyalty and respect. Industry expert Bruce Keslar says that in this business, "everybody seems to believe in kickbacks. I didn't believe in that. I've done this for 32 years on old-country values."

- Remember your vendors at holiday time with a tasteful gift. Something they can display with your name as a reminder works well.

- Find a way to make sure your vendors know when they get business through you. You can follow up with a phone call, or ask the client to mention your name.

5.3.6   Being Your Own Supplier

Over time, it's useful to build up your in-house inventory of party props and supplies. This will allow you to charge the same amount of money to the clients, but with more money revenue going directly to you rather than suppliers — or alternately, you can offer more competitive rates. Since many party planners specialize in a niche service, the items in each planner's list will be different. However, many in the business agree that there are a few essentials to have in your inventory.

Many party planners use their talents to design and make the party props that are used to create a party atmosphere. While creating your own props is a great artistic outlet, there are also some practical reasons for getting out the sewing machine and glue gun.

Making your own props allows you to be more individual with the overall look of your parties. Rented or purchased props are often mass-produced, giving the room and the tables a generic party feel. Clients and their guests want to be at a special party, not the same one they go to every year, and homemade props help them to achieve this feeling.

What's more, it's often difficult to find props and party supplies that match the décor and color of venues. By making props yourself, you can customize the color and style to coordinate with any venue's décor. Also, by making props at home, party planners can turn this creativity into a profit, as any money that the client would have spent to buy props can go directly into your pocket.

Here are a few supplies that the party planners we interviewed discovered were relatively inexpensive and convenient to make or store at home. And at the end, you'll find a list of items our planners suggested you'll want to exclusively rent.

Party Decorations

What's a party without decorations? It's a good idea to always keep some generic party decorations on hand. These can be used several times, and will allow you to decorate ahead of time if possible. They will also save you the time and money required for running to the party supply store before each event.

Maybe the most important decorations to have on hand are seasonal and holiday supplies. There's no mystery what the themes will be near Thanksgiving and Christmas, or on Valentine's Day and Easter. These decorations can be bought off-season to save money, and they can be stored and brought out for each event.

Party decorations vary in price and quality, but a good estimate is to expect to have a minimum of $200 to $300 worth of decoration and supplies on hand.

Centerpieces

All elegant tables have a centerpiece as the focal point, and many party planners insist that this is the number-one item to have in an inventory. It's also one of the easiest items to make on your own.

As centerpieces can literally be made of anything, cost will vary. However, if you're buying complete centerpieces from a supplier, expect to pay anywhere from $5 to $50 a piece. If you're making your own, you can buy supplies in bulk, which saves money and can bring your per-piece price down to a range of $5 to $30.

The base of a centerpiece can be anything, and can be filled with various items to match the theme of your party. Just think of a boat centerpiece with two candles representing smoke stacks for a nautical-themed party, or a glass bowl full of sand with tiny umbrellas and wicker mats for a beach-themed party.

> TIP: Create a new centerpiece for each party that you throw. Use the same base, and change what it holds according to different needs.

If you are planning to make your own centerpieces, there are plenty of affordable places to get the materials: arts and crafts stores, dollar stores, hardware stores, and the list goes on. Remember that a centerpiece does not have to be made of expensive material to get the desired effect.

Flatware and Dinnerware

Although you may rely on caterers or venues to supply flatware, it's a good idea to own a complete set for a couple of reasons. One is that you'll be able to supply smaller parties yourself, which opens up options for you supplying the food. Two, it gives you peace of mind if the flatware being supplied isn't up to your standards, or the supplier simply doesn't have enough for everyone at the party.

A medium-range, 24-setting, stainless steel flatware set consisting of various forks, knives and spoons will cost between $80 and $150. The great thing about owning flatware is that it's easy to store, and you'll have it, in most cases, for life.

Having a good, complete set of dinnerware allows your clients to host a sit-down or buffet dinner anywhere, anytime. This is important for party planners who plan parties and events outside of banquet halls, which often supply these. It also may allow you to reduce your catering costs. A 30-piece set of dishware, including plates, cups, saucers and bowls, starts at around $100.

Linens

Table linens and napkins are great to have for precisely the same reasons as owning dinnerware. There are many different styles and fabrics to choose from, so prices will vary, but one good tablecloth starts at around $30, and commercial linens can be purchased in a set of 18 for around $125. Cloth napkins start at around $5 a piece. Don't forget to factor in the cost of laundering.

Coffee Urn

How many times have you held a party at home and wished that you had a bigger coffee maker? Owning a coffee urn will allow you to provide the coffee at any event. Stylish coffee urns that make 45 cups start at around $100.

Gift Bags

There are many companies that specialize in designing gift bags and do an amazing job. But like centerpieces, this is an item that, with a little creativity, party planners can do on their own.

What first comes to mind when thinking about gift bags are the "goodie" bags given at children's parties. And children's parties are still a big market for gift bags. But there are many occasions, such as Christmas parties or corporate functions, where gift bags are handed out to guests.

Putting together gift bags starts with purchasing the bags, adding gift items, and making the bag more ornate with tissue paper and ribbons. What goes into the gift bag will often be the client's decision and based on budget. But there will also be occasions where it's up to you to decide on how to spend gift money.

Planners Tell Us What to Rent Instead

While building a supply of party props through purchase and your own creativity has its place, there are some items that party planners agree should almost always be rented rather than purchased and stored.

Tables and Chairs

The sheer bulk of tables and chairs makes storing them in your home or office difficult, if not impossible. Although you may get a request for tables and chairs when hired to put on an outdoor or residential event, most venues will be well equipped.

Sound System

The type of sound system needed in order to be heard at most parties and in many venues requires much more wattage than your portable home stereo. It has to be loud, and this usually equals large. If you hire a DJ, they will of course supply the sound system. Many emcees also travel with their own sound system.

Tents

Tent sizes vary, but in order to cover all the food and the guests, they tend to be very large and very heavy, and it takes an entire crew to set one up. The manpower needed alone makes this item worth renting. Party tents are also expensive to purchase, and bulky to store.

Lighting

If your client's party has specific needs, such as a spotlight or multi-colored flashing lights for dancing under, then it's best to rent these items. The high cost and technical complexity of lighting systems means that owning a system is not cost-effective for many party planners, not to mention the fact that they may not be used often enough to get your money back.

Security and Parking Barriers

Wooden and fabric barriers, parking cones, and appropriate signage can be found at local rental outlets.

Name Tags and Table Cards

Many clients will want to have some type of tag or card present at their party, either a name tag that guests wear, or table cards that designate seating arrangements, or tags that tell guests what each item is at the buffet table.

When responsible for providing name tags, many party planners use a commercial printer. However, with the quality of today's home printers, or even just with a creative hand, you can design and deliver the requested name tags with ease. All you really need is some good quality paper, a printer, and some user-friendly software. The software that can be used to make tags is generally the same software used to make business cards at home.

5.4   Setting Your Fees

What you charge clients may look simple once it's nailed down. But the fact is that there are many variables to arriving at that number, including your local market and economy, what other party planners are charging, and the quality and type of service that you offer. This section will look at ways to help you determine what to charge clients, the different ways to charge, as well as how to collect your fees and invoicing.

5.4.1   Factors That Affect Pricing

The city or town where you run your party planning business – and the surrounding areas – will generate most, if not all, of your business. Knowing what factors in your local market affect what you can charge for your services will help you arrive at a price that both returns profits and meets client expectations.

Local Economy and Demographics

Your local economy will play a big factor in what you can charge for planning a party. For example, a town that relies on one large employer that just had a major layoff may mean that there is still a market for parties, but that clients won't have the money to spend on elaborate decorations and elegant appetizers. If the local economy is booming, however, and people have a lot of disposable income, then the opportunity to charge at the high-end with confidence that you're not pricing yourself out of the market will be there.

The best way to know and understand your local economy, its top players, and its potential future growth is to read the business section of your local newspapers and business magazines, and watch business television. Inc.com has a database of information on the economies of several U.S. cities at **www.inc.com/bestcities**.

Demographic research is valuable information for pricing your services. For example, if you open your business in a college town, there's excellent potential for plenty of business; however, they may not host the type of party you can charge a lot for.

If you live in a city or town with a large middle-class made up of baby boomers and their families, your prices may not be a factor when throwing lavish birthday, graduation or anniversary parties. Many baby boomers are busy and have more money than time.

Your Services

As noted in an earlier section, the level of service, as well as the type of service that you offer, determines the type of clients that you attract and work for. But it's also a key factor in what you can charge clients.

Simply put, the more that you do for a client, the more you can charge. For example, if you handle every aspect of the party, from sending out invitations and arranging the meal, to being present at the party and ensuring that it's cleaned up and left the way it was before the party, you can charge a higher rate than a competitor who provides only entertainment.

What Other Party Planners Charge

What your competition is charging may be the most important factor in setting your fees. Why is this so important? The reason is simply that if you're charging too much, you may price yourself out of business. If you charge too little, you either won't make enough profit to sustain your business, or people will think your service is inferior and will be reluctant to hire you.

Finding out what other party planners charge can be done by asking people you know who have hired party planners what they were charged. Also, you can try to phone your competitors and directly ask them what they charge. Some will be forthcoming with the information, while others won't.

During the course of writing this book, several party planners were interviewed and provided information on what they charge clients. To help you in your quest to determine the right price for your party planning services, here are three real-life examples of what party planners from different parts of North America charge.

> EXAMPLE A:
> Big-city, full-service party planning
> *10 to 20% of the overall party budget, or $50 to $150 an hour*

> EXAMPLE B:
> Medium-sized town, full service, provides the meal (no caterer)
> *10 to 20% of overall budget, or $25 to $50 an hour*

> EXAMPLE C:
> Small to medium size town, entertainment only
> *$50 to $85 an hour*

As you can see, rates will vary according to services and location. Also note that if charging by the hour, it is perfectly acceptable to require a minimum number of hours to book your services. Deciding how to charge your clients is the topic of the next section.

5.4.2   Ways to Charge Your Fees

As you saw in the examples, party planners charge their clients in different ways. This section will look at the different methods of charging, and which ways are best for different types of parties.

Hourly Fee

Charging by the hour is a payment system that we're all familiar with, and one that is fairly common in party planning. The general rule for deciding to charge by the hour is based on size and budget. That is, if you're dealing in parties and working with clients who have a smaller total party budget, then you are more likely to charge by the hour.

It really boils down to basic math. Take for example an anniversary party with a total budget of $1,000 that you will spend at least 5 hours directly working on. A 10% fee will net you $100, whereas 5 hours at $40 will earn you $200.

It is also not uncommon to build a minimum-hours stipulation into your contracts, such as charging 2-5 hours minimum. Your hourly fee will likely be anywhere from $20 and up, depending on the factors listed earlier in this section.

Be aware that clients don't like to be surprised with a bill for 20 hours work, when, in their minds, they saw everything only adding up to 10 hours work. The best way to prevent this is to provide an estimate on the number of hours, either at the initial meeting or in the contract, or to guarantee a maximum number of billable hours.

To manage an hourly rate, keep a working ledger of each task that you perform for the party, and the amount of time spent on each item. This will not only assure clients that you are in fact putting in the hours being billed for, it will also help you to more accurately provide estimates for future projects. Below is a *Sample Ledger* you can adapt for your own use.

Sample Ledger

Date	Task	Time Spent	Status	Total Time
Nov. 5/06	Drove downtown to meet with caterers to discuss menu	4 hours, including travel time	Caterer will have samples by next Thurs.	4 hours
Nov. 6/06	Went to select and purchase party supplies	2 hours, including travel	Purchase candles and DVDs for screening	2 hours

Percentage of Party Budget

Another common method of charging for party planning is by a percentage of the total cost or budget of a party. As noted earlier, this can be anywhere from 10 to 30%.

Clients like percentage fees because there shouldn't be any surprises. And party planners like it because it's a no-nonsense type of arrangement that matches the effort to the scope of the party. What's more, for large, expensive parties, it can be a very lucrative way of billing — just think of a 20% commission on a $20,000 party!

A possible setback when charging a percentage fee is underestimating the total cost of the party. To prevent this, you have to be diligent with your budgeting and get all quotes from vendors in writing. You can't be afraid to approach the client with changes to a budget that you've grossly underestimated. Everyone makes mistakes, and there should be a way to resolve the issue. However, in some cases it might be in your best interest to take a small loss (and only a small loss) rather than present the client with "nickel and dime" changes. You'll have to use your best judgment.

> **TIP:** For smaller or budget parties where a percentage of the budget is not enough to be worth your while, you can still gear your fee to the size of the party by charging per number of guests, in the range of anywhere from $10 to $50 per head.

Corporate vs. Individual Party Pricing

Many party planners have a different fee scale for corporate clients versus individuals throwing birthday and anniversary parties. It's not uncommon for a party planner to set corporate fees at least 10% higher than other fees.

The reason is that corporations not only have the money to spend on large parties and a top-notch planner, but the sheer volume of people that they're throwing the parties for means that the parties will naturally be more work. Also, many vendors and suppliers are willing to provide discounts for corporate parties, as the high volume means better economies of scale, and work at a high-profile event.

> **TIP:** Our planners suggest that it's best to charge corporations a percentage of the budget or a flat fee (explained below), as their budget is more likely to be set in stone.

Flat Fee

Some party planners charge clients a flat fee for their party services, although this approach is probably the least used in the business. The reason for its limited use is that a flat fee leaves party planners more vulnerable to underestimating time and money.

Party planners most likely to use a flat flee are seasoned veterans who have budget estimation, time management and party execution down to a fine art. They are also party planners who are well known, and have an excellent reputation, and therefore clients don't mind paying a fee that may be relatively high if broken down hourly.

Determining a flat fee charge for a party is based on a combination of the total budget for the party, and the amount of hours that you think you'll put into the party as a whole. For example, for a medium-size party with an overall budget of $5,000, a flat-fee charge might be $750. This should cover any amount of hours put into the party, as well as insuring that you're staying competitive with those charging a percentage.

5.4.3   Getting Paid

Although party planning may be the most fun you've ever had at work, there's still the practical matter of getting paid. Here's a look at the ins and outs of invoicing your clients and collecting your fees.

Invoicing

Party planning is a business in which you do a lot of work in advance of the day of the event, so it's not uncommon to ask for up to 50% of your service fees upfront, with the remaining 50% to be paid after the party.

When 50% of the fee is paid up front, it is necessary to either have an invoice that accounts for both the upfront and final costs, or two invoices that account for each payment. Either way is acceptable, just be sure that all numbers balance, and that both you and the client have identical copies for your records. Also, don't forget to always keep both a hard copy and electronic copy of the invoice for your records.

It's a good idea to present an itemized invoice. This can include prices for each service, or just a list of the services provided, such as "working with caterers," to help reinforce to clients that they are paying for your expertise and service. Your invoice should detail the following:

- Name
- Business Name
- Contact Information
- Invoice Number
- Date
- Recipient
- Services Provided (itemized list)
- Expenses (if applicable)
- Total Cost
- Payment Date
- Late-fee Provision
- Non-Sufficient Funds (NSF) Provision

Collecting Payment

How clients pay you is entirely up to you, but providing customers with a few payment options is always appreciated. For smaller parties, many clients will pay cash, but for larger parties where the total reaches into the thousands, many would prefer to pay by check.

> **TIP:** Unless you have a retail store, renting the processing equipment that allows customers to swipe a credit card is not cost-effective.

Personal checks are a common way to receive payment in the party planning business. If accepting a check, ensure that your bank processes checks in an adequate amount of time in order for you to pay the bills, but also to ensure that the check is in good standing. Some small business accounts are more flexible than personal accounts.

Cash, of course, should always be accepted as payment for your party services. Just be sure to provide clients with a receipt or invoice to record that a cash payment has been made.

Sample Invoice

To:	Client Address City, State, Zip Code	Date:	August 6, 2008

Attention:	Name and Title of Contact Person

Services and Expenses

Item	Price
Party Planner Fee (10% of agreed-upon budget of $10,000)	$1,000.00
Liquor License	$100.00
Parking Fees	$200.00
Less Deposit of 50% (paid June 26/08)	($500.00)
Balance Due:	**$800.00**

Terms

Payable within 30 days. Late payments or NSF checks will be subject to a 5% fee on top of the balance due total. Thank you for your business.

6. Getting Clients

If your business was a party, marketing would be the invitation. Marketing is what invites clients to use your services — and invites them back again. Just as every invitation can be made to fit the party, your marketing plan will be unique to your business.

Which strategies you choose will depend to some extend on which you have more of, time or money. Few party planners use every single one of these methods. It's great to have your marketing eggs in as many baskets as possible.

When you think of marketing, what do you think of? If only advertising comes to mind, you should know that it's just a small piece of the marketing pie for successful party planners. Advertising can get expensive fast, so when your advertising budget runs thin, your marketing imagination takes over. There are plenty of free and low-cost strategies that can be tailored to meet your party planning business needs.

You will develop a "tool box" of marketing strategies to build your business and sell your services. We're going to fill your marketing tool box in this chapter. You can start with the basics, and add others as opportunities arise.

When you look at all the ways you can market your business that are presented in this chapter, don't be intimidated. Most party planners will tell you that referrals are their number-one marketing tool, so all that is necessary is that you do your job well!

6.1 Your Marketing Plan

Ellen Thrasher is the associate administrator for the Small Business Administration's Office of Business and Community Initiatives. She stresses the importance of looking ahead in marketing. "The most important thing is to develop a marketing plan. You want to maximize your results and you want to minimize your costs," Thrasher said.

So, what strategies really work? Party planner Heidi Hiller told us about an interesting discovery she made based on asking new clients how they heard about her. According to her informal survey results, here's what brought in the clients to her party planning business, in order (we'll cover all these strategies in this chapter):

1) Client word of mouth

2) Vendor referrals

3) Internet and print ads

4) Trade shows/showcases

Some party planners groan at the thought of marketing, since they feel like it takes time away from what they really love to do — planning parties. Or they just don't feel comfortable promoting themselves to others, since it feels like bragging. "The sales end has been my biggest hurdle," admits one party planner we interviewed. "I know I can do it; I haven't found one client where I was over my head or not in my limits. But saying that to someone isn't my forté."

Debbie Donley of The Little Guest in California overcame her initial marketing inhibitions when she started her party planning business several years ago. "Marketing wasn't my strong point, but I found a lot of supportive friends and everyone who was excited about it told someone else and passed around my information," Donley said.

"I've worked hard to get it to a level that I don't have to do so much marketing footwork, but I've pounded the pavement for four years." Her marketing efforts are finally paying off with a well-earned reputation.

Planning for marketing can sound intimidating for people whose specialty is parties, not publicity, but there are resources to help. The U.S. Small Business Administration (**www.sba.gov**) have nearly 1,700 locations where people can get free consulting, including Small Business Development Centers at community colleges and universities, Women's Business Centers, face-to-face business coaches and online coaching. Other excellent resources include SCORE (**www.score.org**) and Canada Business (**www.canadabusiness.ca**).

6.1.1   Your Target Market

When you are developing a marketing plan, you will select techniques and messages that will appeal to your target market. If you specialize in high-end dinner parties, you wouldn't advertise in discount-coupon paks that you throw the "best hoedown ever!" Your wealthy clientele is likely not interested in saving money with coupons, and would never refer to their event as a hoedown — so these are wasted advertising dollars.

While that is an extreme example, you will want to take the time to streamline your marketing plan with only messages and techniques that will a) reach and b) appeal to who you envision your client to be.

But *everyone* loves a party, you're thinking. That's mostly true, but as we explained before, being a generalist is not considered a smart way to do business. If you try to be everything to everyone, how will your client get the message that you will understand their unique needs? "When someone is starting in this business, they need a pretty well defined idea of what is it they're selling, and who it is they're selling to," advises Heidi Hiller of Innovative Party Planners. We agree.

Review section 4.1.2's ideas for choosing a niche, if you don't already have one in mind. Simple questions directed to potential customers can identify aspects of service you may not have thought of, and keeping an eye on other markets and the competition could give you ideas about how to conduct your marketing efforts. Answer the questions below on your own, or enlist a close friend or partner to brainstorm answers:

- Who is my customer?

- How can I target and reach that customer?

- What does my customer need and want?

- How will my business benefit my targeted customer's needs and wants?

- What will my unique selling points be?

- Who are my competitors/colleagues? How is their business doing? What can I learn from their marketing efforts or do differently than they do? What are their strengths and weaknesses? What sets them apart?

- What sets me apart?

If you don't know much about your competition, review the websites of other party planners and learn from them. You can use the PartyPop directory, or type "party planner" into the search engine. How are they presenting their business in words? In pictures? Is it effective or ineffective?

What are their selling points? What benefits do they offer their customers? Ask the opinions of a trusted friend or relative to help you evaluate them, and always keep an eye out for interesting new sites.

6.1.2   Your Marketing Message

In addition to targeting a distinct group of consumers, you want to deliver a marketing message that is geared towards your target market. Think about what they need or value, and find a message that addresses these desires. Do they value great service? Cheap prices? Creativity? Beauty? Elegance?

It's worth considering your marketing message, which may encompass a custom-designed logo, a business name, a tagline, and/or a slogan.

Find something that sets you apart. That may be a unique name for your business, or your face associated with your business, or a memorable title for your product or your website.

For her marketing message, party planner Teresa Choate selected the following business name and tagline: "At Its Best Events: When You Deserve the Best." She felt that described her philosophy of party planning perfectly.

"People are worth it, they've put a lot of time into something and I don't want them to be stressed out. I want people to enjoy and get to be with their guests," Choate says.

Party planner Debbie Donley was on a tight budget when she started her business, but she didn't skimp on message. "I got a graphic artist to help me with a really nice logo, and I think that was invaluable. You present it at the level you want to serve," says Donley. (Her logo appears on her sample business materials in this section.)

"I knew what look I wanted. It needed to reflect me, and I wanted to feel comfortable when I passed it out that it wasn't too corny. I wanted it to be professional, stylish and on nice paper. The thing that the customer is holding in their hand is the quality they're going to experience with my service. If it's a flimsy piece of cheap print, that's not a good sign," she adds.

As you develop your marketing tools (we'll review these in the next section), always ask yourself, do your printed items make a good impression? Are they easy to read, attractive, appealing? Do they reflect well on your business?

If you're on a tight budget like Donley, consider trading future party planning services for the services you need. "I traded childcare because that was my background," she says. "One of the kids I was caring for was the child of a graphic artist, and the artist helped me with a logo."

Part of your message should include your standards or philosophy of service. Even if you never say them aloud, you have principles you conduct your business by. Say them out loud. Write them down, and hang them on your wall.

Here are some examples of standards/philosophies of service:

- We always give 110 percent.
- We have a can-do attitude.
- The customer comes first.
- You're number 1 with us.
- We're fair.
- We're honest.
- We do what we say we will.
- We're big on community.
- We love doing business in Klamath Falls.
- We'll deliver a party you'll love and remember.

Be ready to express your philosophy to potential clients, because not only should it drive what you do, but it may actually sell what you do, because it benefits the client. Your standard or philosophy is what you hope your business becomes known for; what you wish to be famous for. It may well be what separates you from a competitor who also plans "nice" parties.

Also, since party planning is such a personal business, remember that how you come across to people is part of your message. Good grooming, business-like dress, a clean car, well-organized notes and papers: these are all things that make a statement about your business. Does everything about you tell your client that you would be the one to trust with planning their daughter's 16th birthday party? First impressions count.

6.2 Marketing Tools

Once you have thought about who your market is and developed a message that speaks to them, it's time to develop the marketing tools that will help you bring the message to the market.

6.2.1 Business Cards

They don't call it your calling card for nothing! Your contact information is too important to jot down on a loose piece of paper. For the thousands of calls they make on your behalf, a professionally printed card will be a great investment.

Simple white business cards with black ink will be the least expensive if you're on a budget. You can jazz it up with a single spot color for a bit more money, or go full-color (also called four-color) if your budget permits. There will be a charge to add your custom logo, if you have one.

You may also want to consider printing your picture on your cards. You'll notice real estate agents do this a lot. Similarly, you are selling a very personal service, and can benefit from establishing a personal connection with your business cards.

Ordering a large batch of cards (500 or 1000) is the most economical way to go, but only order that many if you are certain your contact information will not be changing. Call around office supply, stationery and printing stores for prices. You should be able to get 500 black and white cards for $50 or less, or 500 single color cards for $75. Color cards and those with raised letters or special effects will be more than $100, but when you think about all the ways you can use your card to promote your business, that's not a bad investment.

It's important to proof your card carefully — you are responsible for catching errors in your contact information. Your phone number may only be one number off, but that means all 500 of your cards are utterly useless, unless you want to pen-correct each one (a tacky move for someone like a party planner!).

Don't forget to put your email address on it, and a website if you have one, as more people are making their business contacts by email these days. If you have two different aspects to your business (party planning and wedding planning, for example) you may want to go with two-sided business cards.

On the next page is a sample business card, reprinted with permission from Debbie Donley of The Little Guest special event planning and on-site child care.

Sample Business Card

Debbie Donley
Director

*Creative on-site child care
and special events!*

1861 Lewis Street
Solvang, CA 93463

805-688-1812
805-688-6980 fax

www.thelittleguest.com

The *Little* Guest

6.2.2   Brochures

A stack of brochures comes in very handy, particularly in the early stages of marketing a business. Your brochure is an extension of your business card, with photos or artwork and a bit more information about the benefits of hiring you and the services you offer.

Basic layouts include bi-folds, the very popular tri-folds, and other more unusual formats or special cuts. A brochure in the shape of a party hat? It's doable too, for the right price. Many small businesses start out with a brochure that is easily photocopied, black ink on paper, using line art instead of photos (photos don't photocopy well). This makes it easy to make more, and it also makes it easy to update quickly. You can improve the brochure by using a quality color paper. If you are getting quite a few done, a business printing center will be more economical in the long run than using your home printer.

Another idea is a postcard with one-color ink (black is cheapest); something that can be changed up and sent out easily without an envelope. Check with a printer on size limitations. There are two main postcard options: half-page and quarter-page, based on a standard 8½" x 11" sheet of card stock.

Remember to design a professional-looking, attractive brochure you can be proud of. One party planner we spoke to told us that her brochure was strongly criticized the first time it was sent out: "I had too much information on it, too much writing and too many choices, and not enough visual." (She heeded the advice, and produced a dazzling new brochure.)

You can get multiple bids for printing projects, once you know your specs. You can say something like: "I'd like you to fax me an estimate for printing a brochure. It will be an 8½" x 11" paper, folded into a tri-fold, with printing on both sides of the paper. I'd like figures for 50, 100 and 500 copies; one with black ink only, one with black ink and spot red. I will need to know what your layout charges run. I will have three pictures. I would also like a price for the same amounts but in full color, and I would like to see the prices on a good quality stock and on a glossy stock."

If you have a professional design the brochure and you want to be able to make changes to it yourself at a later time, make sure they create it in a program you have, and give you a copy of the design file. Many times, professional graphic designers work in programs not typically found on the average computer user's desktop.

> **TIP:**   See if you can get a PDF file of your brochure that you can send to people by email — you'll be glad you did. This is a computer file that virtually anyone can open, and they are smaller-sized files that are easy to send.

There are different kinds of mailings you can do with your brochure. Big mailings, where you buy mailing list labels for a neighborhood or income group, can be expensive for a small business, especially since many people don't like junk mail. However, targeted mailings can be helpful for the new party planner. You can send your brochure out to potential sources of referral business as a start, for example.

On the next two pages, you will find a sample two-sided brochure, re-printed with permission from Debbie Donley of The Little Guest special event planning and onsite child care.

6.2.3   Your Portfolio

Your successful parties can tell their story long after the last guest goes home if you take pictures and keep an updated portfolio. Your portfolio can be as simple as a large folder filled with letters, printed material, and photographs, or it can be as fancy as an expensive, leather case.

Bring the kids.

Relax
and
Enjoy!

Now guests and hosts can relax at special occasions with all the children professionally cared for – right on site! Enjoy your wedding reception, party or corporate gathering. Children get their own, expertly supervised, fun domain at your next big event . . . and what to do with all the kids is solved!

Debbie Donley, Director of *The Little Guest*, is a parent herself and a practicing childcare professional. Debbie knows children.

She founded and directed the *Children's Traveling Adventure Club*, a successful, nature oriented, pre-school program for over 20 years. In this capacity, Debbie has acquired a practical, working experience with a vast array of children's resources. She has introduced hundreds of children to the fascinating wonder and benefit of creative play. Debbie will provide your little guests with a memorable experience.

The *Little* GUEST

Child care and entertainment for special occasions

805 688 1812
thelittleguest@syv.com
www.thelittleguest.com

1861 Lewis Street.
Solvang, CA 93463

The *Little* GUEST

Child care and entertainment for special occasions

Sample Brochure — Side #1

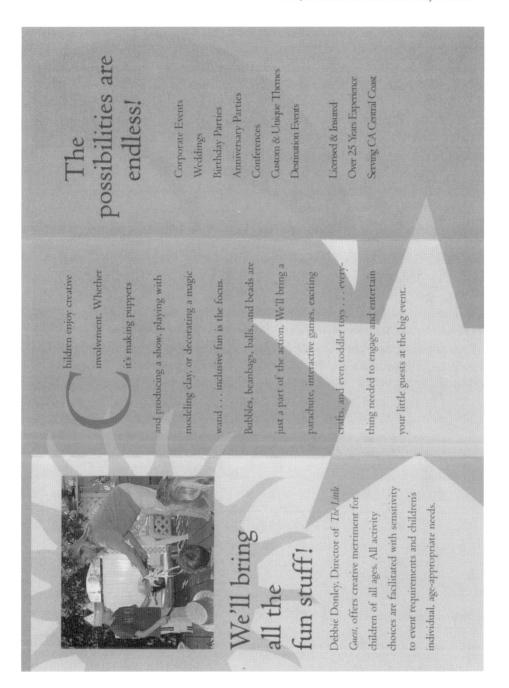

The possibilities are endless!

Corporate Events

Weddings

Birthday Parties

Anniversary Parties

Conferences

Custom & Unique Themes

Destination Events

Licensed & Insured

Over 25 Years Experience

Serving CA Central Coast

We'll bring all the fun stuff!

Children enjoy creative involvement. Whether it's making puppets and producing a show, playing with modeling clay, or decorating a magic wand . . . inclusive fun is the focus. Bubbles, beanbags, balls, and beads are just a part of the action. We'll bring a parachute, interactive games, exciting crafts, and even toddler toys . . . everything needed to engage and entertain your little guests at the big event.

Debbie Donley, Director of *The Little Guest*, offers creative merriment for children of all ages. All activity choices are facilitated with sensitivity to event requirements and children's individual, age-appropriate needs.

Sample Brochure — Side #2

Prepare a cover page for your portfolio. It should be simple and to the point. A printed page with your name, address, phone number and e-mail address is sufficient. This page should be the first thing a reader sees after opening the inside cover.

You can demonstrate your creative flair by using tasteful patterns or hand-decorating the cover page of your portfolio, but be sure to keep it simple enough that it doesn't detract from the contents.

Gather pictures of past events for your portfolio, along with anything else that you think might convince a client to hire you, such as sample invitations you have done, press coverage your events or you receive, or thank-you notes from satisfied clients. Keep your portfolio up to date with only your latest and greatest events.

When you meet with a client for a consultation, have the portfolio ready to view on a laptop or in scrapbook form. "We put together scrapbooks with thank-you notes from our clients and pictures of their parties. We take them with us to the showcases and to meet with clients," says party planner Heidi Hiller.

One party planner we spoke with has a PowerPoint computer presentation that shows what she calls "the anatomy of an event." This is helpful for presentations at trade shows and meetings. She goes through the same presentation in meetings with clients.

6.2.4   A Website

Once a novelty, the Internet has become a surprisingly affordable marketing tool, and increasingly important to the marketing plans of even very small businesses. Pay for it once, update it occasionally, and your website is there 24-7.

"I think it's important to have a website, because I think people get too much stuff in the mail that is difficult to keep up with," comments Sandra Dingler of Party Service in Dallas. Her website, **www.partyservice dallas.com**, is an essential part of her marketing plan.

Party planning is a very visual service, so your website provides the chance to show some samples and the scope of what you do. What makes a great website? "Lots of pictures," says party planner Teresa Choate. "When people are surfing the Web, they want to see photos." Here are other items you can include on your website:

- Present all the same information as is on your brochure.

- Include a form for customers to fill out to get a free estimate. This brings the customer to you.

- To be helpful, offer a tip page with free information about party planning or suggested party themes.

- You can offer brief testimonials from clients you have pleased in the past.

It is particularly important to provide a way for people to get their information to you. Then follow up. This way, your website generates sales leads too.

A website developer can take care of the particulars of building your website. Once you have a website, you've have to spread the word that it exists. Heidi Hiller told us her marketing budget includes fees for a link to her website from the websites of two monthly magazines. "We're not linked all over the place on the Internet, that can get very expensive," she cautions.

Sending E-Newsletters

One possible way to use the Internet to increase your sales is to ask potential clients and existing ones to sign up for an email newsletter on celebrating life's occasions. Send them a weekly, bi-weekly or monthly message with upcoming special dates, handy tips for the season, a tasty recipe or two, or a couple special quotes — things that are useful and enjoyable. It's important to make it friendly and helpful, rather than sales-pitchy, but you can throw in a special offer to encourage them to use your party planning service.

TIP: Be sure you give people a chance to unsubscribe if they don't have time or room in their inbox to enjoy it.

6.3 Paid Advertising

The best thing about advertising your business is that you control the message. Unlike word of mouth, where the information given out may be haphazard, in advertising every word can have a positive spin. You say where the message gets out, what the message says, how the message looks, who gets the message.

It's important to know what advertising cannot do for your party planning business. It's not a magic wand to instantly improve your cash flow. It can't fix the problem if your service is not valued or if it is substandard. Advertising money needs to be invested smartly. Investing 3 to 10 percent of your profits back into advertising is a typical amount, but you should do whatever seems right for your business.

6.3.1 Where to Advertise

One strategy many businesses fall into by default is to ignore advertising because of the expense, but then buy ads on a whim from anyone who calls when things are slow. It's better to be proactive with your advertising.

Call and ask for a rate sheet from publications you see as potential places to advertise, even if you think you can't afford it right away. Ask for some sample issues too. Study the publications and where ads are placed. Frequently, in newspaper, if the price is the same, the back page is a great spot to be in. Be sure to ask when the booking deadline is, and when the copy deadline is.

When you are targeting a specific client – mothers and grandmothers of children under the age of 12, for example – you will concentrate marketing efforts on that group. You have to know the kind of business you want to get and match it up to the market that publication's after.

Bigger publications will have readership demographics for you. Make sure that what you're putting your ad in is going to your audience. Don't just scatter your ads to the wind.

When you think about advertising, you may wish to consider other markets than the traditional newspaper and magazine. "We like to put print ads in school directories, because we do kid things, and those directories have parents for their audiences," one party planner told us.

One party planner found that the phone book yielded surprisingly good results for her. "I put my Yellow Pages listing under 'party planning' and 'wedding/special events.' Being in the phone book is good. I resisted that for a long time," she confessed.

Another party planner cautions that Yellow Pages advertising has its pros and cons. "We've gotten some really phenomenal customers from there, but we've gotten a lot of calls from moms trying to find a clown for a birthday party. We're kind to them, we answer the phone, we're helpful, and we give them some information we can use, but that's not our customer."

6.3.2   Booking an Ad

When you are ready to buy advertising, you need to know what kinds are available. There is display advertising, which runs in a box with a picture somewhere in the magazine; and classified advertising, which are word-only ads that run in the back of the publication.

Generally, businesses use display advertising, although some publications have classified spots businesses can buy. Starting small is okay, but get the biggest ad you can comfortably afford for maximum effect.

Cost Factors

The cost of the ad depends on several things: size, usually measured in inches; frequency, or the number of times it will run; color or black-and-white (color generally costs more in newspapers, but often magazines are always full color); and the publication's distribution.

> **TIP:**   If you don't want to pay for full color, ask your ad rep about spot color. This is when you add one color of ink to your black-and-white ad.

Placement also makes a difference to cost. A front page slot on a daily newspaper is great, but it will cost more. Inside covers of magazines are often more expensive, and the back cover is usually the most expensive with a magazine. These slots are almost always reserved for expensive, full-page ads.

Many marketing experts feel that long-term advertising build name recognition. If you plan on running your ad frequently, let your ad rep know in advance, since they can often arrange a frequency discount if all spots are booked at once. Never commit to a big contract before you see what kind of results you will get with a publication.

Advertising on a Budget

Wherever you choose to advertise, here are some ways to make the most of your advertising dollar:

- Consider a reduced advertising schedule; you may be able to get a frequency discount for a schedule of being in the publication every fourth edition or four times a year.

- Consider timing ad appearances with heavy party-planning seasons, if you are targeting certain times of the year.

- Check to see if they have special editions that may suit your marketing plan: November for Christmas parties, for examples, or February for weddings.

- One party planner says that she teams up with a floral designer friend on advertising. "It seems to work because it shows both of our talents. Event planning is a little hard to show in print, so you just have to show the pretty stuff," she explains.

- Trade your services for ad space. One party planner did trade-out for advertising with local radio stations by providing party planning services.

- One party planner was so pleased with a publication's advertising results that she let her ad rep know. The publication asked her to put it in writing, and then ran the letter as a testimonial, free of charge. "They actually featured us in that ad, and they printed it free several times," she said.

Designing Your Ad

Great advertising is all about the difference between features and benefits. Ads that show and tell how your business benefits your client are better than those that just talk about you.

For example, if your feature is that you are located right in town (compared to a competitor in the next city, for example), the benefit might be that you are local and easy to consult with. You are a party planner: that's a feature. You organize the details; the client doesn't have to sweat the small stuff, because you do that for them: these are the benefits.

When it's time to design your ad, you provide the copy (the words), but a good ad representative will help you plan your ad for maximum impact. They will design it, sometimes with no charge. It helps greatly to have a couple samples of ads of a similar size that you like the look of to show them what you have in mind.

To spend your ad dollars most wisely, tailor the ad to what you accomplish. Don't just let the ad department of the publication "throw something together."

Here are some "awesome ad" tips:

- Don't crowd your ad with too many words, images or ideas.

- Make sure you proof your ad well. Beyond everything else, make sure your phone number is right. Generally, if you proof it and there is a mistake, they will expect you to still pay for it.

- You can use your own picture to increase your recognition in a smaller community.

- "Latch onto the emotional end of the event, the visual, because you cannot show the organizational end in print," says one party planner.

Once you have something that works, you may want to stick with it. "I had a real pretty ad… then I switched to update it and do something else. I switched colors and it definitely didn't have the same appeal," one party planner ruefully told us.

Sample Advertisement

*This ad is copyrighted and appears courtesy of
Innovative Party Planners, LLC.*

The Advertorial

With advertorials, you buy an ad, and you get an article. Have a copy-writer write a story, such as the story of your company and its success, and create an ad modeled after an editorial page. Most publications will insist that if you do an advertorial-styled ad, it must be identified as advertising, at least in small letters. And of course, remember, it is pure advertising, so you will have to pay for it accordingly.

6.4 Networking

Some people get cold feet when the topic of networking comes up. Their palms sweat as they imagine making cold calls or arranging meetings to make sales pitches to people about your services. But networking should be a part of your marketing plan that is casual and enjoyable. Networking is about meeting and interacting with people in the industry or potential clients in either a social or business atmosphere for the purpose of mutual assistance or support. Focus on the word mutual —the relationship should benefit you both.

While some people you meet may have an immediate need for your services (or know someone who does) in most cases you will be laying the foundation for future business. By establishing relationships through networking you can be the one people think of when they do need a party planner.

"One-on-one networking is huge. You get what you put into it. You never know what contact you're going to meet, or what contact will be beneficial to you. People will refer people they know, and it's good to know other businesses in your community," says party planner Teresa Choate.

6.4.1 Who to Network With

If you're a new party planner and you want to get your name known, then you have to get on the collective radar. But you simply will not have the time to network with everyone who might possibly be interested in your services, so confine your attentions to your target market.

Who you network with will depend largely on your target market. If you are marketing to mothers with young children, you need to find ways to infiltrate and be a part of their social groups. You might set up a temporary booth at the mall, or arrange to make a speech about holiday entertaining for the local PTA.

If your market is brides-to-be, you'll want to attend bridal shows. If your market is 20-somethings, you'll want to spend time in nightclubs, college campuses, and hip coffee shops. If your market is local professionals, you could join your local Chamber of Commerce, Kiwanis club or Rotary Club.

People who use party planning services are usually reasonably wealthy. To meet wealthy people, you can attend or volunteer at museum and art gallery openings, or charity and political fundraisers.

Check the Social or People pages of your local newspaper to find events the wealthy attend, or look in the Yellow Pages under "Societies" or "Charitable Organizations." Focus your searches on the wealthier areas of town, and join branches that are local to them. You might see if you can find a way to socialize at a local golf or country club through a friend or colleague, or become a member yourself.

Whatever your market, you'll need a valid reason to interact with them — not just for selling. If you have kids of your own, you can easily meet other parents and sell them your planning services, but if you don't, you have to be a bit more creative — maybe by offering a seminar for parents of children (in a wealthy neighborhood!) on creative gift bags, for example.

Networking with Vendors

An excellent way to get referral business is to make contact with other professionals who are likely to have customers who could use your design services. Contact bridal shops, florists, caterers, etc. Explain your business concept, and ask if you can leave a stack of business cards and/or brochures at their facilities. You might also offer a referral bonus, which can be a percentage (like 5%) of the order, or a flat fee like $25 or $50.

You will need to incorporate networking with vendors into your marketing strategy. When you first start your party planning business, you may not have the advantage of referrals from other party-related vendors. It takes some time to build that up, and an investment of your time, but it can help your marketing efforts pay off.

To get the ball rolling, take one day of the week, get dressed up and visit businesses on your vendor list. Take them out for coffee, find out what they do and tell them what you do.

As we mentioned earlier, meeting vendors and potential associates face-to-face gives them a chance to see you in action, and lets you size up how they respond in a business setting. If a vendor is rude or unhelpful, it could make you think twice about using them in your party planning business. Conversely, establishing a cordial working relationship will impress others in a position to refer business to you.

Focus on becoming very familiar with the industry, on educating yourself not just about what is involved, but who is involved. Meet the other vendors you're going to be working with. To get the cooperative ball rolling, you may offer to do some work with them at a discounted rate.

Getting your business card out there is essential. Getting it out to the party rental places is a good idea. Talk to the manager and ask if you can leave cards or brochures, and get some of theirs. Go back to the florists and the caterers and refill that every couple months, and make sure your card is still visible.

6.4.2 Networking Groups

Ask yourself what groups exist that can help you form valuable business alliances. One of the most popular business networking outlets is your local Chamber of Commerce. Through mixers, after-hours gatherings, and ribbon cuttings and seminars, members create ties that they will rely on in the future when doing business.

In larger urban areas, industry-specific networking groups meet on a regular basis. In Maryland, party planner Heidi Hiller is part of the National Association for Catering Execs, where she has met other vendors and formed alliances. She and her business partner also help with organizing the group's events. "Nobody gets paid to do that but it helps us showcase each other," she says.

> **TIP:** If there isn't a networking group for events specialists in your area, you might even consider starting one. Teresa Choate told us she started a wedding professionals guild in Ellis County.

Teresa Choate is a member of the Waxahachie Chamber of Commerce. "There are a lot of avenues you can take through the chamber for networking. You can volunteer to do things, or help with fundraisers and upcoming events for charities. They always need free things for auctions, and if you're starting out, that's a good way to show your services."

Carol Rejcek of Garden Gate in Ennis, Texas handles corporate and family parties. Her constant involvement in local volunteer efforts has opened doors for her. Rejcek is a mainstay at the Ennis Chamber of Commerce, and with fellow event organizer Nancy Swindell she formed the Ennis Historic Downtown Merchants Association. Her high profile and attitude of service has yielded some interesting and high-profile opportunities. "Being involved is very important to my business," Rejcek said.

Debbie Donley said the flow of business-to-business networking goes in both directions. "I went to women's business networking groups. They all exchange business cards, and they're all in the position of marketing their little business, and everyone's wanting to help each other," she said. "Those relationships are key. If you have people who have faith in you and know you can do it, that helps you get started."

You can find local service clubs by checking the Yellow Pages and your community newspaper, or contacting your local Chamber of Commerce. To find a local Chamber of Commerce in the U.S. check out the Chamber of Commerce Directory at **www.chamberofcommerce.com**.

6.4.3   How to Promote Yourself

Go to as many networking events as possible. When you go to a networking event, don't be a wallflower, and don't just hang out with people you know well. Those people already know you plan parties. Mingle! Look for opportunities to tell people what you do.

When you attend social or business functions with potential clients, you'll want to have plenty of business cards available. When you collect business cards from others, write the occasion and date on the back to jog your memory later.

Don't give people your card before you've had a chance to talk to them a bit, or you'll seem like you are just trolling for business. Exchange business cards only after you've established that the potential for a mutually beneficial relationship exists.

If you meet someone who expresses an interest in or need for some party planning, follow up after the meeting with a glad-I-met-you introductory letter, and send your promotional materials (brochures or postcards) to them. You can give them a call a few days later to see where they are at.

If you are in a social situation where talking about your business may not be appropriate, listen for opportunities to tactfully bring it up. If you want to introduce your line of work to the conversation, a quick and easy way is to comment nicely on the decorating in the room you are in, or the food you are eating. This becomes a natural lead-in to mentioning what you do.

Your Two-liner

You should practice describing what you do briefly and accurately to people. It should flow easily. Your two-liner is the answer to, "So what is it you do?" Here are some examples:

- "I'm a party planner. We do a lot of fun children's parties and family parties, and we organize elegant corporate get-togethers for our clients."

- "I own Short and Sweet Parties. We specialize in workplace parties and events, but we do a lot of family parties and birthdays, too."

- "I own and manage Sharon's Party World. We operate on the idea that every party is special, and we provide turnkey party organization for groups of all sizes. What do you do?"

TIP: Don't forget to ask what they do, too, and then think about if there is any connection between what you do and what they may need. For example, if they say, "I'm a sales manager," you can tell them what an office party can do for staff morale.

Your two-liner should make it sound like you're good at what you do, and that you love it. It should be inviting enough that if the person you're giving it to is at all considering throwing a party, they might be interested in hearing more from you. You might even work your philosophy of service in there somewhere.

How to Close

Before you finish talking with that person you are networking with, remember to make sure they have your card, and invite them to contact you. You can try one of the phrases below:

- "Let me give you my card. If there's any way I can ever be of service, please give me a call. I'll look forward to talking with you again."

- "Do you have a card? And here, let me give you mine. If you need some help with organizing an event, give me a call. We try to keep our services very affordable."

- "I'd like you to have my card. If you decide to use entertainers at that picnic, give me a call. I keep a running list of talent that has done a good job for my clients."

- "I'd like to give you my card. When your school has that fundraiser, please call me. I'm a big PTA booster, and I'd love to donate a raffle item."

6.5   Get Some Free Publicity

Getting the local press to write a story about you is a great way to get business, since stories are often perceived as being more authentic than advertising. Many people will surmise that if the newspaper or local magazine is covering you, then you must do good work. Here's how to catch some media attention.

6.5.1   Write a Press Release

A press release is an article you prepare to give to the press, in the hope of having it covered as news. You can write press releases about things that have happened as well as about things that are going to happen, or general press releases that can be printed any time. "I think having a [general] press release is an important thing," one party planner told us, adding that she updates it frequently, and sometimes tailors it for special occasions.

You can announce your new party planning business to the local publications by sending a press release. (Be forewarned that a pretty typical response to this is that the advertising manager gives these to ad sales reps and says, "Go sell them an ad.") Some newspapers will run the announcement, either in a business notes section or somewhere else.

A successful press release may be printed verbatim, if the editor is willing, or it may be revised. You generally have little or no say whether it gets published at all, although if you are an advertiser in the publication you have better chances. (If you are advertising, send a copy of the release to your ad rep as well to ensure they are aware of it.)

The press release may be accompanied by pictures of a specific event, if the release is about the event, or a color headshot of the subject. Pictures should be of as high quality as possible, and include people. If your press release is about your new business, don't just include a picture of a popular party venue. Put yourself in the picture!

Press releases may be sent to the publication, with hard copy as well as accompanied by a CD of pictures. They may also be emailed, but be sure to get the right email address for the current editor. You can follow up with a phone call to the editor, but don't bug them.

Don't forget TV and radio for upcoming events. On a slow news day, you may get some coverage, particularly if you have a unique angle: your event will feature a parade of clowns or penguins or there will be a famous guest (as long as publicity is welcomed by your client).

Sandra Dingler has had her share of free press. "One time the Dallas Morning News did an article on people who had jobs involving time management. I think one of the people was someone who dealt with freeway grids, one with scheduling the basketball season," she remembered.

The resulting two-page spread featured Dingler and the others. To get the pictures for the piece, the photographer came to a party and followed her around, taking pictures as she went about her day.

If you can't get any media attention for yourself or your events, you can try to be a little more proactive in your approach. Debbie Donley sometimes helps with publicity at events she volunteers at, in addition to planning. "I'd take pictures and make sure they were submitted to the local paper," she says.

TIP: If you are not getting any response to your press releases, consider hiring a copywriter to help you; it could be the difference between getting into a publication or not.

Building a Press Kit

It is good to work towards putting together a "press kit" as you grow your business, in case you get some media attention. Think of it like your portfolio, but for the media. It should include a business card, brochure, basic facts about your business, party tips and helpful hints, good photos of people enjoying your parties, and a good picture of you in color.

Having this on hand in a tidy folder ensures that media who interview you have easy access to correct facts about your business, such as the spelling of your name and your business name. To make it fun, you can put in a party favor or an imprinted item, or whatever you'd like to make it memorable in a nice way.

A *Sample Press Release* appears below. Note the style: contact info at top, suggested headline, date, third person, remarks in quotes. Generally, two pages (double spaced) is the maximum length. Of course, remember the five W's: Who, What, Where, When, and Why.

Sample Press Release

FOR IMMEDIATE RELEASE   August 21, 2008

NEW BUSINESS IN IPSWICH
Penny Whistle opens Parties With Pizzazz

Ipswich entrepreneur Penny Whistle has opened Parties With Pizzazz, a party planning business serving communities around Ipswich County. Whistle is familiar to many in the Ipswich community for her involvement in Keep Ipswich Beautiful, and as the longtime president of the Ipswich PTA.

She said the decision to start the company grew from her hobby of catering parties for friends. "I have always enjoyed organizing events for other people, and I had received many compliments on the parties I helped create. When my children became school-aged, I decided to put my creativity to work full time to help others with their events," she said.

Whistle provides party planning services for corporate and family events. She specializes in providing children's entertainment areas at larger local venues. "The Pine Mist Winery has been using my services for a while. Whenever they have a large event, I provide a fun and safe party environment for the children of attendees," she said.

She plans to work closely with local vendors who provide catering and party rental services, she said. "I think it's very important to support local businesses, because everything we need is right here in Ipswich County. It's a great place to be in business," she said.

For additional information, contact Penny Whistle at (555) 444-3333.

#

6.5.2 Be Seen As an Expert

There's nothing like self-promotion, and one of the best ways to get your name out there is to establish yourself as an "expert source" for information. Journalists use experts in their stories every day, but they don't always have time to search for them. There are all kinds of opportunities that may come up, such as these ones our experts have contributed to:

- An article on how to throw a Super Bowl party

- An article on having a 15-minute party in the office

- A story on what party planners do for their own children's parties

Does your community have a local access cable station with local shows? That's one place for guest TV appearances in party-giving seasons. When dealing with the media, avoid giving one-word answers. Look for ways to provide great sound bites — paragraphs that give a positive statement on a relevant topic.

Planner Sandra Dingler publishes a monthly citywide calendar of events to establish her expertise in the industry. "We turned it into a way to keep track of non-profit activities that affected social people," she says. "It's just a public service more than a moneymaker, but people certainly know our name, and a lot of people have our phone number because of that."

If you like to write, don't wait for the journalists to come to you. Consider writing a column or article for a local publication. If a magazine has a section on entertaining, suggest an article on seasonal party planning, for example.

Ask how many words they need, and then stick to it. Use their publication's style, looking at other articles that have run, and include your "mug shot" with your submission. (If you don't want to write it, you can pay a copywriter to ghost write it for you.)

One party planner we spoke to has had several articles she has submitted published for free, using topics like tips for handling children at your wedding. It's good for business because it positions her as an expert, and the editor appreciates fresh local copy.

When you are the expert in an article, take off your "sales" hat and put on your "expert" hat. People want to hear helpful tips in articles, not to be ambushed by sales jargon. The editor will usually allow a tagline at the bottom of the article: "Becky Lindthorp is a Muscle Shoals party planner. She can be reached at blindthorp@yourserver.com."

Also, have a nice color picture of yourself for publicity photos, or for use on your brochure or business card. You may make it a glamorous portrait, or a very good photo of you in your party planning element. Say cheese!

6.6   Other Marketing Strategies

Here are some other ways to get some attention for you and your fledgling party planning business. You can see which ones are a fit for your style and scope of services.

6.6.1   Donating Your Services

Your soft heart may be one of your best marketing tools. Even though you make a donation to be helpful or because you believe in a charity's cause, the good news is that helping out can score you marketing points in the community. In the beginning, giving away some of your services will help get you known. For the most part, it costs you your time and energy instead of your money, and as everyone knows, when you start a business, sometimes you have more time and energy than you have spare cash lying around.

The events themselves make opportunities for referrals. When guests notice the splendidly set tables, the program running like clockwork and the impeccable overall service, they will ask who arranged this wonderful party.

Think about the events that go on in your community all year. Charity auctions, luncheons, walk-a-thons, business networking groups such as Rotary, Lions and Kiwanis, the Chamber of Commerce, golf tournaments, school fundraisers, church bazaars — all of these need door prizes and raffle or auction items.

How about donating a children's party package? Or a centerpiece, or a pony ride package, or whatever you specialize in and can donate without breaking the bank? Or go in with vendors to create a total package that's worth more and gets even more attention.

For example, you might donate a "cowboy barbecue" to a Chamber of Commerce auction, in partnership with a horseback riding vendor and a restaurant or caterer to offer horseback rides and a chuckwagon-style meal of barbecue brisket with all the trimmings. The idea will fire up the imaginations of bidders, and get a great deal of attention for the businesses.

Volunteer, donate a party package or do party organization at cost for the causes of your choice. You may get a word of praise from the podium or a place in the program, or even a mention in the newspaper. But besides those kudos, people will talk, and the talk will be good. You'll be connecting with others who either need your services or can refer them to others.

6.6.2   Promotional Items and Signs

Innovative items imprinted with your name or logo can be a great way to lodge yourself in people's minds. You can get your identity branded on everything from mugs to rulers to magnets, which can in turn be used as gifts and prizes.

Debbie Donley made her good-looking logo work for her in the public eye. "I got a logo printed on my shirt and on my apron, so every event we do, our logo is repeated and seen by everyone," Donley said. Sandra Dingler has her own note cards printed up along with her business cards, and slips a little personalized note in with every invoice and every check. She also had a special folder printed up for pictures that she shares with her clients after the event.

There are inexpensive alternatives too. "When I do an industry fair, I take a little something cute they could take home and keep," explains Debbie Donley. On one occasion she bought packs of little party-size Play Dough to give out, putting her own sticky label (which she had printed up by the thousands) on it.

If you don't have a business location with space to advertise, signage may not be a concern. There are some ways to get around that, though. Debbie Donley settled on an automotive show-and-tell. "I tried magnetic signs and they would keep falling off. I got a personalized license plate that said 'L'GUEST,'" she said, adding that people do make the connection to her business, The Little Guest.

One party planner found a party rental place she frequently used allowed her to hang a sign outside their place that had her business name and phone number. The 4' x 6' sign is double-sided and hangs under the main sign for the business. It cost her $150, a great one-time investment.

While her business isn't in a primo downtown location, planner Heidi Hiller lucked out with the location she and her business partner chose after outgrowing their office in her partner's basement.

"We are in a business park near where people have to get their car emissions inspected, so every two years everyone has to pass by our door," Hiller said. "We have so many people that come in and say, 'I just saw your sign.'"

6.6.3   Offer Additional Services

There is also the potential to increase business by adding value by offering additional products and services. Just as some caterers and designers move into the planning business, so it is possible to grow the business in the other direction.

One method would be by expanding vertically — that is, by expanding the range of services you offer in-house. Thus instead of contracting out design, invitations, and/or catering to vendors, you might bring those operations under your control.

In addition to your party planning services, you could generate additional revenue by offering for sale products that you create yourself or by reselling items that you purchase at wholesale prices. These could be offered as stand-alone items or promoted along with your party planning services as an adjunct to the event.

For example, you could offer custom gift baskets or gift bags that reflect the theme of the party and incorporate elements of your designs into the baskets. They can be as simple or elaborate as you like, but be sure that you charge enough to make such a side-venture profitable. This means covering your costs, including what you paid for the items as well as the time you spent creating them, and making a profit above that.

6.6.4   Trade Shows

If you're seeking a way to generate sales leads, meet a lot of potential customers in one place and on one day and to have potential customers come to you, consider trade shows. The trade show is a very visible (if temporary) business venue, from which you can personally meet with clients and suppliers.

Generally these are more available in urban and suburban areas, sometimes called expos or expositions. That's a great word, and it has the same roots as the word "exposure," which is the reason you take your business to an expo.

These are often held at the same venue year after year, and sponsored by the same organizations. Check with your Chamber of Commerce, publications or convention center for a schedule to consider which upcoming trade shows might be most beneficial to you.

Even small towns have ways to make a trade show presence. Having a booth at a school fair or an expo hosted by a non-profit organization can get you some of that meet-and-greet, show-and-tell interaction with the public. It's personal — a condensed opportunity to shine and to be seen.

Your goals for the trade show are two-fold. You want to present your business to potential clients, and generate leads for future follow-up. You can use extra incentives to lure passersby to your booth where your work will be on display. Consider a draw for a party for 10, a bouquet of balloons, or just some item that would be appealing. Have a bowl for people to drop their business cards in, or small tickets for them to enter their name and phone number. Follow-up after the trade show is essential, because that's the only way to make leads pay off.

Since you are showcasing your work, use the resources available to you as a party planner and your creativity in particular. One party planner used a tiki hut design to create an inviting booth, adding lighting and a festive tropical air to make it memorable. She became known for the booth, and showcase attendees would return year after year, and bring friends.

Instead of standing behind your table at the booth, try standing in the middle of the aisle. Don't pressure passersby like a perfume-spraying salesperson. Have something to give out, like business cards or giveaways, or brief entry forms for a giveaway. If they linger a little longer, ask some questions. "The friendly, helpful, informative sales approach has really gone a long way for us," one party planner said.

7. Conclusion

You have reached the end of the *FabJob Guide to Become a Party Planner*, but hopefully this is a new beginning as well — of your career as a professional party planner. Don't be intimidated by the success of others you meet and read about. You will build your own great reputation just by doing a great job for your clients.

"In Washington, D.C. there are a lot of party planners, but you see certain names over and over again because they become associated with a certain standard of work," Ellen Thrasher told us.

Word of mouth will play a huge part in your initial success as a party planner. Referrals and repeat business are the easiest sells. Your top referrer is a happy client. Impressing your client is free.

The most important thing you can do to build your business is to be reliable and follow through on your commitments. Do what you say you are going to. Do a great job on each party. Then ask for their business again, and ask for their referrals.

Carrie Katz of Creative Parties by Carrie in Thousand Oaks, California got the ultimate word-of-mouth compliment at a party, when a woman approached the party host and complimented her on the fabulous event.

"You are unbelievably calm, what is your secret?" the guest asked.

"Carrie," the host replied simply.

Cheers, and have fun being the secret behind each great entertainer's success!

More Guides to Build Your Business

Increase your income by offering additional services. Here are some recommended FabJob guides to help you build your business:

Get Paid to Plan Weddings

Imagine having an exciting high paying job that lets you use your creativity to organize the happiest day of people's lives. **FabJob Guide to Become a Wedding Planner** shows you how to:

- Plan a wedding ceremony and reception
- Select reputable vendors and avoid disasters
- Get a wedding planning job with a resort, tourist attraction or other wedding industry employer
- Start a wedding planning business, price your services, and find clients
- Plan your own wedding like a professional wedding planner
- Be certified as a professional wedding planner

Get Paid to Plan Special Events

Imagine getting paid to use your planning skills to organize a variety of events including corporate meetings, conferences and large public events. **FabJob Guide to Become an Event Planner** shows you how to:

- Teach yourself event planning (includes step-by-step advice for planning an event)
- Make your event a success and avoid disasters
- Get a job as an event planner with a corporation, convention center, country club, tourist attraction, resort or other event industry employer
- Start your own event planning business, price your services, and find clients
- Be certified as a professional event planner

Visit www.FabJob.com to order guides today!

Increase Your Profits with Catering

Your clients could hire you to provide catering services for their parties and corporate events. The **FabJob Guide to Become a Caterer or Personal Chef** shows how to:

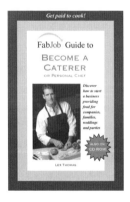

- Set up a professional kitchen and plan menus
- Obtain food service equipment and whether to rent, buy, or use disposables
- Start your own catering business, work with food suppliers, and hire service staff
- Start your own personal chef service supplying meals for busy families
- Market your business, set your prices, and do client consultations.

Get Paid to Work With Flowers

As a floral designer or flower shop owner, you will be surrounded by beauty every day, and you will have the opportunity to use your creativity to brighten people's lives with flowers. The **FabJob Guide to Become a Florist** shows you:

- How to identify and care for popular flowers, greens and plants

- How to make flower arrangements for weddings, funerals and other occasions (including step-by-step instructions)

- How to get hired as a floral designer

- How to stat your own flower shop, find suppliers, set prices and attract customers

Does Someone You Love Deserve a Dream Career?

Giving a FabJob® guide is a fabulous way to show someone you believe in them and support their dreams. Help them break into the career of their dreams with more than 75 career guides to choose from.

Visit www.FabJob.com to order guides today!